Vision of the Empyrean
Gustave Doré (1832–1883)

9 CIRCLES

BY **BILL CAIN**

★

★

DRAMATISTS
PLAY SERVICE
INC.

9 CIRCLES
Copyright © 2013, Bill Cain

All Rights Reserved

SPECIAL NOTE

9 CIRCLES was developed at the Ojai Playwrights Conference,
Robert Egan, Artistic Director and South Coast Repertory's Pacific Playwrights
Festival, Martin Benson and David Emmes, Producing Artistic Directors.

Winner of the 2010 Sky Cooper New American Play Prize at Marin Theatre
Company, where it received its world premiere under the leadership of
Jasson Minadakis, Artistic Director and Ryan Rilette, Producing Director.

2

For Patrick J. Adams

*Knowing that Patrick is around to act impossible parts
gives me the confidence to write them.*

AUTHOR'S NOTE

Stories are my way of understanding the world. I think that's true for most of us. We can understand an event if we can fit it into a story — so we must be careful with our stories.

I was five when I was first introduced to one of the stories that shapes our world on a daily basis. Since it was the first movie my parents ever took me to see, it made a tremendous, foundational impact on me. It was an allegory about a coalition of the Good who defeat absolute Evil with the help of God and brutal, murderous violence. It was called Walt Disney's *Snow White and the Seven Dwarfs*. It is the children's version of a story that shapes a great deal of our understanding of the world.

It is Shakespeare's national philosophy — Harry V decimates the evil French and it is God's victory, not ours — so this primal story shapes a good deal of our political thinking. As it is Milton's theology — God battles Satan in cosmic war in *Paradise Lost* — it shapes a good deal of our religious understanding. This take-no-prisoners good-versus-evil battle consumes an enormous percentage of the Bible. There are no tears for Goliath. What a relief then for me to meet — better late than never — Dante and his alternative view of the universe — *The Divine Comedy*.

If you haven't read it, you have a great treat in store. It is great fun, very moving and, above all, it provides an alternative story framework for understanding our lives — political, religious and personal.

Life is not a battle, but a journey. The hero is not a lonely man on a solitary crusade. He is always accompanied by a guide and mentor — one who is willing to go through any and every fire with the traveler. The ultimate goal is not the obliteration of the enemy. In Dante, when you achieve your crown, it is not because you have conquered the world; it is because you have become "lord of yourself."

And heaven and hell are not so far apart. In *The Divine Comedy*, they are adjoining territories. To get to one, you have to pass through the other. Although some of the people you meet in hell are undoubtedly evil, many are not. There are many good, beautiful, unlucky people in hell and a great many mediocrities on their way to heaven. One of the joys of the journey is Dante's surprise in finding that he has good friends in both places. There are sympathetic moments all along the way. And there is compassion for the damned. At the very center of hell there is terrible violence, but the ones perpetrating the worst of it weep as they do it.

Above all, there is the woman. In the Bible, woman is the flaw in creation. Eve, the weaker vessel, ate the apple and we all suffer. In Dante, Eve — with Mary, Ruth and Beatrice — holds the key that unlocks the ultimate mystery.

At the end of the *Comedy*, you reach not a bloody battlefield, but a vista full of blinding light where you can see what you have always hoped for — the love that moves the universe.

Like *The Divine Comedy* after which it is modeled, the soldier's journey in *9 Circles* is a journey through terrible darkness into transforming light. In some of the darker scenes, it is important to remember this.

(Incidentally, it is also important to remember that — even at his darkest — Dante finds humor — as does Reeves — as do we.)

The first production of this play at Marin Theater Company ended with an extraordinary moment.

As the soldier stood perfectly still, the world changed around him.

Craig Marker — our Reeves — stood in a light cue that grew gradually over the course of his final seven-minute monologue. As the intensity of the light grew, the moment became a transfiguration.

I mention this moment — created by Kent Nicholson (director), Michael Palumbo (lighting and set designer), Callie Floor (costumes) and Craig Marker (Reeves) — because it so perfectly illuminates the journey of this play. As the nineteen-year-old Reeves learns and grows in each circle, as he accepts his own — and our own — darkness, he is illuminated from within.

As for many of us, it is not the darkness within that is unbearable, but the light.

9 Circles is ultimately a journey we make together towards that demanding, revealing light.

Bill Cain
Fall, 2010
Marin

9 CIRCLES received its world premiere production in 2010 at Marin Theatre Company in Mill Valley, California. It was directed by Kent Nicholson; the set and lighting design were by Michael Palumbo; the costume design was by Callie Floor; the sound design was by Cliff Caruthers; the stage manager was Angela Nostrand; and the dramaturg was Margot Melcon. The cast was as follows:

REEVES . . . . Craig Marker
LIEUTENANT, ARMY ATTORNEY, PASTOR,
LAWYER, DEFENSE . . . . James Carpenter
YOUNG FEMALE LAWYER, SHRINK,
PROSECUTION . . . . Jennifer Erdmann
Understudy . . . . Aldo Billingslea

9 CIRCLES was also produced at Bootleg Theater in Los Angeles, California. It was directed by Justin Zsebe; the set was by Jason Adams; the lighting design was by Lap Chi Chu; the costume design was by Kathryn Poppen; the sound design was by Adam Phalen; the stage manager was Amber Koehler; and the assistant stage manager was Johnny Rodgers. The cast was as follows:

REEVES . . . . Patrick J. Adams
LIEUTENANT, ARMY ATTORNEY, PASTOR,
LAWYER, DEFENSE . . . . Paul Dillon
LIEUTENANT, PASTOR . . . . Joe Holt
YOUNG FEMALE LAWYER, SHRINK,
PROSECUTION . . . . Arlene Santana

CHARACTERS

DANIEL EDWARD REEVES — 19/20 — an American soldier in Iraq and after.

(The other roles should be played by two men and a woman. It is possible to do the play with only one man, but two are preferable.)

MEN:
LIEUTENANT

ARMY ATTORNEY

PASTOR

CIVILIAN LAWYER

DEFENSE

WOMEN:
YOUNG FEMALE LAWYER

SHRINK

PROSECUTION

Note: The cast members will announce changes of place and time throughout. Circle titles that appear in bold are not read aloud.

9 CIRCLES

CIRCLE 1: HONORABLE DISCHARGE

*Daniel Edward Reeves — an army private for less
than a year — nineteen — maybe twenty — Texan — enters.
Lean. Intense. Standing at rigid military attention. This
young man desperately wishes to remain a soldier.*

The woman appears — like the men, in military fatigues.

She carries a pair of army boots.

WOMAN. CIRCLE ONE: IRAQ. HONORABLE DISCHARGE.
*(Before exiting, the woman will place the boots down as an emblem of the
scene. In each scene, an emblem of the scene will be placed on stage. An
army lifer lieutenant — 30 — enters — with Reeves' orders in his hand.)*
LIEUTENANT. Private REEVES.
REEVES. Sir!
LIEUTENANT. Your orders.
REEVES. Sir.
(Lieutenant opens orders. Reads. Then —)
LIEUTENANT. *(Happy for Reeves.)*
Honorable — discharge.
(As the lieutenant goes to sign the orders —)
REEVES. Honorable discharge? I don't like the sound of that, sir.
LIEUTENANT. You like the sound of "*dis*honorable discharge"
better?
(Lieutenant goes to sign.)
REEVES. *(Don't sign.)*
At least it means something, sir. You know something happened
and it wasn't good. "Honorable discharge" sounds — bad.

LIEUTENANT. Bad? In what way?

REEVES. Sexual.

LIEUTENANT. "Honorable discharge."

(Lieutenant gets it.)

REEVES. Sounds like what your biology teacher'd say 'cause he's not supposed to say "cum."

LIEUTENANT. A euphemism.

REEVES. Is that where the words mean the opposite of each other?

LIEUTENANT. *(No.)*

That's oxymoron. Military intelligence. Euphemism. Like somebody who wouldn't say shit if he had a mouth full of it.

REEVES. Yes, sir. That's it exactly, sir. Sir, I want to stay here until we win this war, SIR.

LIEUTENANT. Son, if we could've won this war, we would have won it at the Battle of Lepanto.

REEVES. When was that, sir?

LIEUTENANT. Before your time.

(Preempting objection.)

Private, you've got no say in the matter.

(He goes to sign the orders.)

REEVES. *(To delay the signing out.)*

I'll desert. I'll learn their language. I can already count to ten. I'll join them. I'll become their leader. Like in that movie.

LIEUTENANT. *(Intrigued.)*

Lawrence of Arabia? Peter O'Toole.

REEVES. *Universal Soldier*, sir. Jean-Claude VanDamm.

LIEUTENANT. Son, you know why you're being discharged?

REEVES. I know what the form says, sir. It says I have a personality disorder, sir.

LIEUTENANT. And what do you think of what the form says?

REEVES. I think — I think it's a euphemism, sir.

(Then.)

I'm no expert, but I think a personality disorder can be an advantage in certain circumstances.

LIEUTENANT. Such as?

REEVES. Some things don't bother me the way they bother other people.

LIEUTENANT. Like?

REEVES. The basics, sir. Killing people. It bothers some people, sir.

LIEUTENANT. It doesn't bother you?

REEVES. Sir, we came here to kill people, sir.

LIEUTENANT. *(Gung-ho.)*

Soldier, we came here to help build a nation. That is our mission. Operation Iraqi Freedom. And that's a very unusual expression because it's both a euphemism AND an oxymoron. You don't see a lot of them but when you do, run, because it means there are no words to describe the unspeakable fuck-up you are in.

REEVES. *(Gung-ho-er.)*

Sir, I don't mean we're here to kill *all* the people. Just the ones who hate freedom. Whoever is left when the killing stops — that's the nation.

LIEUTENANT. Son, I don't know why they're sending your home. Seems to me you're everything we want in a soldier. *(Checking his file.)*

You're nineteen?

REEVES. Yes, sir.

LIEUTENANT. Your home's Texas, right?

REEVES. Wherever these men are is home for me. They're my brothers, sir.

LIEUTENANT. You know the French Foreign Legion? They take an oath, but they don't take it to their country.

REEVES. That's because the French are fucked up, sir.

LIEUTENANT. They take their oath to the Legion — to one another — they kind of avow themselves to one another. This isn't that.

REEVES. No?

LIEUTENANT. No.

REEVES. Army of one, sir?

LIEUTENANT. What do you think of that, private — army of one?

REEVES. Army of *one?* It's an oxymoron, sir.

LIEUTENANT. You know, for a grunt, you're pretty smart.

REEVES. That was not the consensus of opinion of the faculty at my high school, sir. I'm not smart, sir, but I can learn if someone will show me.

LIEUTENANT. It says here you sought help —

REEVES. *(Twitch/wince.)*

That was the mistake, wasn't it, sir?

LIEUTENANT. Maybe not. You've seen some terrible things. You've seen people die.

REEVES. That doesn't bother me, sir.

LIEUTENANT. No?

REEVES. No, sir. People are *supposed* to die, sir.

LIEUTENANT. Bodies like meat don't bother you?

REEVES. No, sir.

LIEUTENANT. No?

REEVES. I mean "No, not like meat, sir." *Meat* gets cut on the joint.

LIEUTENANT. Bodies like hamburger then?

REEVES. No.

LIEUTENANT. Bodies like *what* then?

REEVES. *(A moment, then —)*

Like a couch.

(Then.)

A leather couch in a nice house. And they took good care of the couch.

LIEUTENANT. Who?

REEVES. The people who live in the house.

(Then.)

It cost more than they could afford. It cost more than anything they ever bought. Maybe it cost more than their car. But one night while one of them was sitting on the couch —

LIEUTENANT. Who?

REEVES. Doesn't matter, sir, we're talking about the couch — one night somebody breaks in and stabs the person on the couch.

LIEUTENANT. Who breaks in?

REEVES. A freedom-hating raghead breaks into the house and stabs her and she's surprised.

LIEUTENANT. She?

REEVES. She/he — doesn't matter, sir. What matters is that he didn't have time to get off the couch. *He* stayed on the couch until *he* bled out. And even though they do everything they can to make the house clean again, the realtor can't sell it because something bad happened in the house.

LIEUTENANT. On that couch.

REEVES. *(No.)*

The couch is gone. The couch gets put in a lot. A vacant lot. Vacant except for the couch. It's a good couch, but not even junkies will sleep on it.

LIEUTENANT. Because of the blood.

REEVES. Because of the blood dogs come and tear it apart.

LIEUTENANT. What kind of dogs?

REEVES. You're right. Coyotes, sir.

LIEUTENANT. You've got quite an imagination, son.

REEVES. They think the couch is meat because it has blood in it, so they tear into it but they can't find the living part. They tear into it every time it rains because, every time it rains, the blood gets wet and it's like the couch is trying to come to life but it can't because it isn't anything anymore. Not even a couch. That's what the bodies look like, sir.

LIEUTENANT. You're right. That's what they look like.

REEVES. And you look at your friend's legs and you're embarrassed because they don't even look like meat anymore. He's torn open but you don't see the inside of his body. You see the inside of the insides. Not muscles, the inside of muscles. Not bone, the inside of bone. And that's very private stuff. Not even God ever saw stuff like that. But your friend he's waving it around like he's got no shame and he's screaming and crying and you're sort of embarrassed because this guy — this guy who'll never be anything anybody will ever want again — not even as much as somebody wants a good couch in a nice house — he doesn't know enough to die? *That* bothers me.

LIEUTENANT. You know Jackson? His legs got torn apart. Just like you say. Torn right off and a hunk of his arm gone like a shark bite. Just like a shark came up and took a piece out of him.
(Then.)
He's back. It took courage, but he's back.

REEVES. Yes, sir, I know. That's what makes me so —
(Reeves can't speak.)

LIEUTENANT. Talk to me.

REEVES. *(Torn between rage and sorrow.)*
So you're telling me a guy who was torn to pieces — *he* can get back here — and stay here — and you're telling me what's *in here* —
(Reeves' head.)
WHAT'S — INSIDE — HERE —
(Fighting tears.)
— is in WORSE SHAPE — than a guy who was TORN TO FUCKING PIECES BY A PACK OF DOGS AND A SHARK? Is that what you're telling me?

LIEUTENANT. No, son. Nobody's saying that. What's wrong with you — it might be something small. But whatever it is — all they're saying is — it can't be fixed.
(Then.)

Dismissed, soldier.

REEVES. Sir! I took an *oath,* sir. It's not just the French Foreign Legion. We take oaths too.

(Then, truth —)

I, Daniel Edward REEVES, do SOLEMNLY SWEAR I will SUPPORT AND DEFEND the Constitution of the United States AGAINST ALL ENEMIES, FOREIGN AND DOMESTIC; that I WILL BEAR TRUE FAITH and allegiance to the same; and that I WILL OBEY THE ORDERS OF THE PRESIDENT OF THE UNITED STATES and the orders of the officers appointed over me, according to regulations and THE UNIFORM CODE OF MILITARY JUSTICE. SO — HELP — ME — GOD. So help me God the first time I said it —

(Moved.)

I knew it was the truest thing I ever said. Do not make me break my oath.

LIEUTENANT. A minute ago, you were going to join the enemy.

(Reeves works on it. Then —)

REEVES. Infiltrate.

LIEUTENANT. Infiltrate.

REEVES. Infiltrate. Not join. I'll volunteer to be a suicide bomber. I'll strap on a vest and in the middle of my going-to-Allah party, I'll pull the pin and blown them all to hell.

(Then —)

Joking, sir.

LIEUTENANT. You're an articulate son of a bitch. I'll give you that.

(Reeves laughs.)

REEVES. Sorry, sir. Things come together in my head sometimes and I laugh inappropriately, sir.

LIEUTENANT. What was funny?

REEVES. Me — articulate, sir.

LIEUTENANT. What's funny about that?

REEVES. My job description, sir.

LIEUTENANT. What's that?

REEVES. I'm a GRUNT, sir.

LIEUTENANT. Not anymore. You're discharged. Honorably.

(Signs.)

Your war is over, son.

REEVES. *(Gung ho.)*

Request permission to keep my uniform, sir.

LIEUTENANT. Son, you can keep anything that isn't stamped Property of the U.S. Government.

(Reeves checks the inside of his cap. It's the government's. He hurls it to the ground. Checks his jacket. The government's. Damn! Hurls it to the ground. As transition music plays, he checks all of his clothes until he is naked on stage.

As the uniform comes off, it's almost as if Reeves loses his bone structure along with the clothes. And his will to live. But that might be the fact that he is coming off a very committed three-day drunk.

He ends up in a police station — T-shirt and flip-flops — out cold.)

MAN. CIRCLE TWO — UNITED STATES OF AMERICA. SOME MONTHS LATER. HOLDING CELL. PUBLIC DEFENDER.

(The man has been holding an empty beer bottle. He places the bottle on the stage before exiting.)

CIRCLE 2: HOLDING CELL

Young female lawyer (YFL) — business suit — enters the cell and looks for Reeves.

Reeves is out cold on the floor of the cell.

YFL. Mr. Reeves.
(Nothing.)
Mr. Reeves.
(Losing patience.)
Mr. *REEVES.*
(Reeves starts awake. Looks around.)
REEVES. Where am I? ... Man, I hate waking up and not knowing where ...
(Completely hung over, he looks around at his surroundings. Sees the Young Female Lawyer.)
Oh.
(Then, back to sleep.)
I want a lawyer.

YFL. Mr. Reeves, I am a lawyer.

REEVES. I mean a *real* lawyer.

YFL. I am a real lawyer.

REEVES. Really? You *look* like a public defender.

YFL. Well, I am a public defender.

REEVES. Great. Just great. Nothing personal. It's just — tell you the truth — I've been through this before.

YFL. Well. To tell you the truth — I haven't.

REEVES. Great. Fucking great.

(Reeves farts satisfyingly. Shrugs. Goes back to sleep.)

YFL. I am fully competent to get you through the arraignment. Then you're done with me and you can hire whatever lawyer you want.

REEVES. I got no money and a beat up car. How can I hire any lawyer I want? You. You're my lawyer. You're my — defender.

YFL. Tomorrow, Mr. Reeves — Mr. Reeves? — Mr. Reeves, all you have to do tomorrow is watch for me to nod my head and, when I do, say in a loud clear voice — Not Guilty.

(She starts out.)

REEVES. Hey, defender. Defender! I can't lose my license.

(He's embarrassed about needing the car. Not-giving-a-shit-entirely would be real freedom. However — the truth is —)

I *need* the car.

YFL. Mr. Reeves. In all probability — you will never drive a car again.

REEVES. That's a mean thing — just — what a *mean* thing to say.

(Then, getting it.)

OK. I'm sorry for what I said about public defenders. OK? Now — worst case. *Worst* case. What kind of time am I looking at?

YFL. You are looking at the death penalty, Mr. Reeves.

REEVES. The death penalty? For a DUI?

(Then.)

Even a public defender — even a lame public defender — ought to be able to get less than the *death penalty* for a DUI.

(She does not respond.)

This isn't a DUI, is it?

(Then.)

What did I do? Did I get in a fight? Did I black out? I didn't hit somebody with the car, did I?

(No.)

Whatever. I was drunk. I had the right to be. I don't know why *everybody* isn't drunk. You know why I was here?

16

YFL. You were here for — for the funeral.
(Impressed.)
I understand you served with him?
REEVES. *(Bragging.)*
Him? *Them.* I "served" with all *three* of them. Funerals in Texas, Oregon and Arlington.
(Shaking off the hangover.)
Can't go to them all. I thought — Arlington ought to know how to do a funeral. Don't get me wrong, it was nice, but —
YFL. *(With some awe.)* Texas.
REEVES. You saw it?
YFL. On the news.
REEVES. People every twenty feet. Everybody holding flags. For miles. Not bad for a dropout who pumped gas. He just got married. You know that? He didn't tell his folks. Just us.
YFL. Eighteen. She was —
REEVES. Eighteen. Hell, he was —
(Bizarrely bragging.)
It's — *my* — *fault* he's dead. Hell, it's my fault *all three of them* are dead. If I had been there …
YFL. You think you could have protected them?
REEVES. *(Not exactly.)*
I make people nervous. People get — careful — when they're around me.
(Then.)
You feel a little careful around me? Don't you?
(Silence, then —)
Well, they *needed* to be *careful.* If they'd let me stay over there, those soldiers would still be —
(Twitch-wince, then —)
What the hell. GUILTY. I was drunk. I was driving. Whatever happened, it's my fault. Plead me guilty.
(The professional emerges in our Lawyer —)
YFL. Mr. Reeves, there are only two words I want to hear from you and "my fault" are not those words. Say "my fault" to the judge tomorrow and you will me make look like I didn't do my job— like I didn't defend you — for a public defender, that's *bad.* Two words.
(Cuing.)
Not — ???
(Reeves is getting to like her.)

17

REEVES. Not guilty. OK?

(Yes.)

Hey, what did I do? What am I "not guilty" of?

(She takes out paperwork.)

REEVES. No. Just — your own words — that's all.

YFL. You should hear the charges again.

REEVES. Again?

YFL. *Listen* this time.

(Then —)

One. *On or about April 16, 2006, outside the United States, to wit, in Iraq — while a member of the United States Army —*

REEVES. Wait … Iraq?

(Yes.)

Iraq?

*(*Very *puzzled.)*

I didn't have my car in Iraq.

YFL. Would you like me to start over?

(No.)

While a member of the United States Army subject to Chapter 47 of Title 10 of the Uniform Code of Military Justice — the defendant, Daniel E. Reeves, did, with malice aforethought, unlawfully kill a person, an Iraqi man by shooting, an offense punishable by more than one year if committed in the special territorial jurisdiction of the United States, all in violation of Title 18, Section 7 and 3261(A)(2).

(Silence. Then —)

REEVES. *(Completely unconcerned.)*

Hell — they're not going to take my car away for that.

(Then — with a building edge —)

YFL. Two. *On or about April 16, 2006, outside the United States, to wit, in Iraq —*

REEVES. *Iraq* — did I kill people over there?

YFL. *— while a member of the United States Army —*

REEVES. You bet I did.

YFL. *Subject to Chapter 47 of Title 10 —*

REEVES. How many?

YFL. *— of the Uniform Code of Military Justice —*

REEVES. Nowhere near enough.

YFL. *The defendant —*

REEVES. You want to know what I plea?

YFL. *Daniel E. Reeves did —*

REEVES. Guilty.

YFL. — *with malice aforethought* —

REEVES. Kill people?

YFL. — *unlawfully kill another person. An Iraqi* —

REEVES. *That's what I was supposed to do.*

YFL. An Iraqi woman.

(Then — from memory.)

An offense punishable by more than one year if committed in the territorial jurisdiction of the United States in violation of Title 18, Section 7 and 3261(A)(2).

(Silence. Then, sizing up the situation —)

REEVES. You're not a *regular* public defender, are you?

YFL. Federal.

(Silence. Then, deeply puzzled —)

REEVES. How can what happened *over there* be a crime *over here*?

YFL. *(No clue.)*

Like I said — I've never been through this before.

(Then.)

Three. On or about April 16, 2006 —

REEVES. Cut to the —

YFL. *Daniel E. Reeves did unlawfully kill* — *an Iraqi child.*

(A moment. Then — sobering up —)

REEVES. I made a mistake over there. Fisher. Fisher did it right. I should have done what Fisher did.

YFL. Fisher?

REEVES. Oregon.

YFL. What did he do?

REEVES. He *died* over there. You know what they did to him? You see the video?

YFL. Yes, I saw the video.

REEVES. They cut off his head.

YFL. *(Enough.)*

I saw the video.

REEVES. THAT's why people are lining the streets. That's what makes him a hero. He got his head cut off. The mistake I made was coming home alive.

YFL. Well, you may get your wish yet, Mr. Reeves. People are most definitely out for your head.

REEVES. *(Realizing —)*

Fuck. *Everything* we did over there is a crime over here.

YFL. *(Becoming personal.)*

Mr. Reeves? We're at war. Terrible things happen in a war. I know that.

REEVES. You know that?

YFL. *(Even more personal.)*

Terrible things happen. Yes, I know that. I believe — under the right circumstances, anyone — *anyone* — is capable of terrible things. I think that's why I became a public defender.

REEVES. No, that we're at war. You know *that?*

YFL. Yes.

REEVES. How? How do you know that?

YFL. How do I —

REEVES. I mean it could be like the moon landing. Couldn't it? Do you think we landed on the moon? Really. Do you?

YFL. Mr. Reeves. Daniel —

REEVES. Do you?

YFL. Yes, we landed on the moon.

REEVES. We landed on the moon? We did?

YFL. Yes.

REEVES. You think *you* — any *part* of you — landed on the moon?

YFL. Well … no.

REEVES. So *we* didn't land on the moon. You're pretty sure of that? You pretty sure you didn't land on the moon?

(Yes, then, violently.)

Then how can you be *so fucking sure we're at war? You're* about as much at war as you are on the *fucking moon.*

YFL. I mean the country is at —

REEVES. The *Marines* are at war. The *Army* is at war. The country? You know what this country is fighting?

(She doesn't.)

An obesity epidemic!

(With vast contempt.)

Now what fucking Iraqi accused us of —

(Reeves grabs the papers from her.)

Who wrote that? Who —

(Reading.)

SOI1 was interviewed and explained that —

(Then.)

SOI1? Who the hell is —

YFL. SOI. Source of Information. It was in a stress debriefing.

REEVES. A stress debriefing? Iraqis don't get —

YFL. It was an American soldier. Talking to a counselor.

REEVES. An American? Soldier? Said?

(YFL takes the papers —)

YFL. *SOI1 explained that SOI2, SOI3, PFC Daniel E. REEVES and KP1 —*

REEVES. KP1?

YFL. Known Participant 1 … *were conducting duties at TCP2 —*

REEVES. Traffic Control Point 2 —

YFL. *— 200 meters from the residence where the crime occurred.*

(YFL creates the event —)

Prior to departing TCP2, SOI1 —

REEVES. *In your own words.*

YFL. *(This is hard.)*

Well — it says Private Daniel Reeves and several of his squadmates — currently in the brig in Iraq — went to a house. There Private Reeves herded an Iraqi man, woman and child into the bedroom where he shot and killed them. Then he went into the living room where two of the soldiers were holding a woman down and he raped then killed her. Afterwards, they set her body on fire.

(Then.)

I don't know why they call her a woman. She was fourteen.

(Silence. Then —)

REEVES. Do you think we did this? Is that what you think?

YFL. Terrible things happen.

REEVES. *(Astounded.)*

YOU THINK WE — ? WE don't DO things LIKE THIS. *Insurgents* did this. We *investigated* it. That report — it's *nothing* but *lies.*

YFL. Perhaps. Still, there is something to be learned from it.

(A moment, then —)

There is only one name in this report. In this whole report, there is only *one* name.

REEVES. Daniel E. Reeves.

YFL. Exactly.

(With some sympathy.)

Daniel, you are going to need a lawyer — not only a real lawyer, an extraordinary lawyer — to get you through this — but for tomorrow, you are innocent until proven guilty.

(As she goes —)

REEVES. You're going to help me, aren't you?

YFL. I'll get you through tomorrow.

REEVES. Tomorrow? Tomor — ?

YFL. A lawyer will be appointed for you, Mr. Reeves.

REEVES. By who?

YFL. The government.

REEVES. Wait a minute. Who wants me dead?

YFL. The government.

REEVES. Well, that's not good. Is it?

(Reeves laughs out loud. Inappropriately.)

YFL. Be careful what you say tomorrow. Two words. "Not guilty,"
Mr. Reeves. "Not —

REEVES. *(Fuck you.)*

Two words. "HONORABLE — DISCHARGE." You think they
give honorable discharges to people who —

(A name is called —)

VOICE (MAN.). Daniel Reeves.

(At the sound of his name, YFL leads Reeves into court.)

VOICE. How do you plead? … Mr. Reeves — guilty or not guilty?

(YFL looks to Reeves. Nods.)

*(Reeves' brain jams with a thousand things he could say. He shakes
them off one after the other. YFL nods again. Nothing. Then —)*

YFL. Mr. Reeves will not enter a plea at this time.

VOICE. Are you represented by counsel?

(No response.)

Mr. Reeves?

(Reeves laughs inappropriately. Then —)

REEVES. Judge, do you think we went to the moon?

(Silence.)

VOICE. Counsel will be appointed.

REEVES. What about my car? I need the car! I need the car!

*(Gavel. YFL moves for the exit. Reeves is stripped of his civilian clothes
and is redressed in an orange jumpsuit. Before YFL leaves —)*

YFL. *(To audience.)* CIRCLE THREE — A HOLDING CELL —
PRIOR TO TRANSFER TO FEDERAL PRISON. PAIN OF
THE ENEMY.

(She leaves the charges she has read on the floor and exits.)

CIRCLE 3: JAIL

Reeves — now in orange jumpsuit — is pissed off at himself and the world in general.

REEVES. *(Over the top.)*
GUILTY! GUILTY! I meant to say, *"Hand me over* to the Iraqis. *Let them* bury me up to my neck in sand and *stone* me to death. *Televise* it. I'll sing *'God Bless America'* till I'm dead and people will see what I'm made of and who those fucking people are."
ARMY ATTORNEY. Tell me, Mr. Reeves — does that work for you?
(Army Attorney — military uniform — enters. Rank: Captain. Presentation: Military perfection. Education: Princeton. Third-generation military.)
REEVES. What? Does what work for me?
ARMY ATTORNEY. That act.
REEVES. Act? What act?
ARMY ATTORNEY. "Let them bury me up to my neck in sand and stone me to death." Does it work for you? Because it will *not* work in your trial.
(Reeves looks him over, then —)
REEVES. Who the hell are you?
ARMY ATTORNEY. Someone who would very much like to represent you in your trial, Mr. Reeves.
REEVES. An army lawyer. How stupid do you think I am?
ARMY ATTORNEY. I'm a good lawyer, Mr. Reeves. I have won cases against the government. I got a man out of Guantanamo.
REEVES. Yeah, whose side are you on?
ARMY ATTORNEY. Yours. If you'll let me be.
(Reeves is unsure. So — nonchalant bravado —)
REEVES. Well, between you and me, I've decided not to worry too much about the trial. Innocent until proven guilty, right?
ARMY ATTORNEY. Mr. Reeves, you have already been tried and convicted.
REEVES. What?
ARMY ATTORNEY. The only thing still in question is the sentence.

Not even the sentence — only the manner of its execution. *Your* execution, Mr. Reeves.

REEVES. What…? What'd I miss? They've had me locked up pretty tight here and I — Did I miss something?

(Army Attorney puts hat, briefcase on chair. Surveys room while schooling Reeves.)

ARMY ATTORNEY. You were arrested the third —

REEVES. Thursday.

ARMY ATTORNEY. The next night — July 4th — the President of the United States went on television and spoke to the nation about you.

REEVES. *(Happily surprised.)*

He did? … About —

ARMY ATTORNEY. He said you were a stain on the United States' honorable image.

REEVES. Well, that's not right.

ARMY ATTORNEY. The next morning —

REEVES. Yesterday.

ARMY ATTORNEY. General Pace went on television —

REEVES. Who?

ARMY ATTORNEY. You used to work for General Pace, Mr. Reeves. He's the head of the Joint Chiefs of Staff. He said 99.9% of America's fighting men and women serve with honor. You were a dishonorable exception.

(Preempting Reeves.)

There were "allegedly's" in all the right places, but everyone knew what they meant. They meant you're guilty, Mr. Reeves. Of capital crimes.

(A moment. Then — bravado —)

REEVES. Anybody else talk about me?

ARMY ATTORNEY. The President of Iraq wants you handed over to Iraqi justice.

REEVES. *(Showing off.)*

Iraqi justice. Oxymoron.

(Reeves impresses himself. But —)

ARMY ATTORNEY. You're a bit of a disappointment to me, Mr. Reeves. I was expecting someone smarter.

REEVES. I'm smart. People are always telling me how smart I am.

ARMY ATTORNEY. Would you like to know what you are, Mr. Reeves?

(Then —)

You are a Texas boy brought up in a single-parent home. Your father spilt early so you grew up alone with your mother in The Back of Beyond, Texas.

REEVES. Is that in my file?

ARMY ATTORNEY. Just a guess. Stop me when I'm wrong. You did what you could for her — your mother. You tried to help out. My guess is that she relied on you as the man of the house.

(Silence. Then —)

REEVES. Maybe.

ARMY ATTORNEY. That's a kind of incest, Mr. Reeves.

REEVES. Are you saying — are you saying I slept with my —

ARMY ATTORNEY. It doesn't matter. Either way, she made you her Man. Because you were confident of your Manhood at an age when everybody else was learning to tie their shoes — nobody could get to you. Am I right, Mr. Reeves?

REEVES. *(Yes, so, defensive —)*

Didn't anybody teach you not to talk about somebody's mother?

ARMY ATTORNEY. *(Thought so.)*

Teachers, coaches, cops — they all tried to wake — you — the — hell — up before you did something destructive of self and others but they couldn't because you thought you were The Man when all you were — all you *really* were — was your mother's anger at men.

REEVES. Well, that ought to be worth something in a court of law.

ARMY ATTORNEY. I would never bring that into court.

REEVES. Then why are we talking about it?

ARMY ATTORNEY. Because I want you to know I know who you are. I want you to know that you are not going to manipulate me like you manipulated those men — good men probably — in your squad. You got them to kill and to rape —

REEVES. Allegedly.

ARMY ATTORNEY. — and you did it easily —

REEVES. *Allegedly.*

ARMY ATTORNEY. — because that is what you were trained to do —

REEVES. *Allegedly.*

ARMY ATTORNEY. — by basic training that was a lot more basic than anything the army could devise.

(Stone cold anger —)

REEVES. How did you do at basic? No, don't tell me. Stop me

when I'm wrong. Let me guess. You sucked up everything the army threw at you and asked for more. I bet you were great. Look at you. You ARE the army. You know what, Army? You know how I got here. You TOOK me. It was you or jail and you fucking took me. *(Bitter, driven truth.)*
You know what the recruiter said to me? He said, "Son, this will be a new start for you." You know how much I wanted to hear that? I thought fuck — maybe they can *beat* something new into me. Maybe they can nail me onto a tank and drive me into battle. You know what they did in basic? They *advised me of my rights. Rights?* I didn't *want* any fucking *rights.* I wanted somebody to fucking tell me there was no way but their way. Fuck! THIS —
(The cell.)
— is what the ARMY was *supposed* to keep me *out* of. Well, FUCK THAT. *I kept MY END of the BARGAIN.*
(A moment. Then —)
ARMY ATTORNEY. *(Entertained.)*
That … That's what I mean. Does *that* — work for you?
REEVES. WHAT?
ARMY ATTORNEY. That — *act.* Do you ever drop it or are you West Texas bullshit to the core?
(Consideration. Then — pleased —)
REEVES. It got me where I am today.
ARMY ATTORNEY. And where is that?
REEVES. Heads of state are fighting over me.
(Smile.)
ARMY ATTORNEY. Goodbye, Mr. Reeves.
(Gets hat, briefcase. Leaves.)
REEVES. Bye. Tell the army I fell for their bullshit *once* and I won't —
ARMY ATTORNEY. *(Stopping.)*
Oh … No … The army didn't send me. Officially I'm not even here.
REEVES. Say what?
ARMY ATTORNEY. I'm here on my own, Mr. Reeves. On a hunch.
REEVES. Hunch? What hunch?
ARMY ATTORNEY. You aren't what I was expecting, Mr. Reeves. And it was a long shot at best.
(Army attorney sees Reeves as a lost kid for a moment. Sincerely —)
ARMY ATTORNEY. Good luck.

(Then, as he leaves —)
REEVES. Hey, Army. You know I got baptized? During basic.
ARMY ATTORNEY. *(Checking watch.)*
No. I didn't.
REEVES. No act. No bullshit about it. I prayed. I prayed to be a soldier.
(A moment.)
Fuck. I prayed to be you.
ARMY ATTORNEY. I'm not the answer to a prayer, Mr. Reeves.
I have a very ordinary life. Wife — house — kids.
REEVES. Ordinary, huh? You're fucking clueless.
ARMY ATTORNEY. Everyone has a destiny. You have yours.
REEVES. Right.
ARMY ATTORNEY. Mr. Reeves —
(With respect.)
You scared them.
REEVES. Say what?
ARMY ATTORNEY. You scared them, Mr. Reeves.
(Then.)
The Supreme Court doesn't scare them. Congress doesn't scare them.
The death of the young does not scare them. I would have said nothing could, but you, Mr. Reeves, you put the fear of God in them.
REEVES. Who?
ARMY ATTORNEY. Heads of state.
(Reeves wonders if he's being mocked.)
REEVES. *(Absurd —)*
You think that a general is scared of a fuck-up from Midland, Texas?
ARMY ATTORNEY. Yes, but not you.
REEVES. Of who?
ARMY ATTORNEY. The other fuck-up from Midland, Texas.
(Then.)
And I think that *other* fuck-up is afraid — very afraid — of you.
(Then.)
If this had happened in Midland, Texas, they wouldn't have cared. But it didn't. It happened in the middle of their war and you have scared them, Mr. Reeves. You tore the war open. You did the unimaginable.
(Clueless. So —)
REEVES. I got a good imagination.
ARMY ATTORNEY. *(Indeed you do.)*
You performed an act so unimaginably cruel that — for a second —

you made them feel the pain of the enemy. It scared them and rightly so. If you were to do that for the country, you could end the war.

REEVES. If this war could end, the battle of Lepanto would have ended it.

ARMY ATTORNEY. What do you know about the battle of Lepanto?

REEVES. Not much. It was before my time. Go on.

ARMY ATTORNEY. They don't want this war to end, so they need to make you go away and they usually get what they want. So, take your pick, Mr. Reeves, lethal injection or stoning.

REEVES. *Those* are my *options?*

ARMY ATTORNEY. There might be another. Mr. Reeves — I would like you to consider re-enlisting.

(Consideration. Then —)

REEVES. Man, the army must be having some *serious* trouble meeting its quota *this* month.

ARMY ATTORNEY. I need to know if you're willing. It affects the options for your trial, Mr. Reeves.

REEVES. You're not kidding. Are you?

(Army attorney does not kid.)

ARMY ATTORNEY. If you re-enlist, you would be tried by a military court.

REEVES. The army threw me out.

ARMY ATTORNEY. An honorable discharge isn't getting thrown out. The military can return a soldier to active duty.

REEVES. Why would they?

ARMY ATTORNEY. There are some in the military who feel this war is a brutal misuse of resources. They might be willing to accept you to get jurisdiction in your case.

REEVES. But why —

ARMY ATTORNEY. There is a question about the war that should have been asked before this war began. They would like to ask it now in the only way they can — in a military court. A federal court won't tolerate it.

REEVES. What question?

ARMY ATTORNEY. "Is it worth it?"

REEVES. The war? Is it worth — ?

(Offended.)

We were attacked. People — people got *killed.*

ARMY ATTORNEY. Yes, they did. Do you know how many?

28

REEVES. What does it matter how many?

ARMY ATTORNEY. 3,000.

REEVES. OK, 3,000. *3,000 Americans got killed. Somebody* has to pay.

ARMY ATTORNEY. 40,000 Americans get killed in *traffic accidents* every year.

REEVES. So?

ARMY ATTORNEY. Based on your logic, we should be bombing car dealerships. To avenge 3,000 deaths, we have lost 5,000 soldiers. It makes no sense. There are those in the military who would like to point that out.

(OK, so —)

REEVES. What would you say?

ARMY ATTORNEY. No more than what you said a moment ago. The army knew what it was getting when it took you. You have drug convictions. No high school diploma. No employment record. They had to lower every requirement they have to get you in. They had to give you a morals waiver. In most states you wouldn't be allowed to own a gun and yet —

REEVES. Wait a minute. You're going to say the army is fucked up because I'm *in* it?

(No response.)

You're going to say I never should have been in the army?

ARMY ATTORNEY. I think I can get you life, Mr. Reeves.

REEVES. Everything I did before the army? Everything since? Shit. The army was my life. I had ten months of life. What's the point of getting "life" if I can't hold on to the only part of it I ever cared about?

ARMY ATTORNEY. Mr. Reeves, life matters to *everyone.*

REEVES. Your life, maybe. Lethal injection. Have the doctor put me to sleep and then — sweet dreams.

ARMY ATTORNEY. No doctors are involved, Mr. Reeves. In fact, no medical personnel. They take an oath to do no harm.

REEVES. So who — ?

ARMY ATTORNEY. Amateurs. It isn't pretty. And it is entirely possible that death by lethal injection is excruciating. But nobody knows, because — well, who can you ask?

(Then.)

Sodium triopental puts you to sleep and then pancuronium bromide paralyzes you so everything that follows *looks* peaceful, but? If you are

29

not actually asleep — and who's to know after the paralysis sets in — or if the amateur crew injects the potassium chloride into a muscle rather than a vein — you might be awake — trapped — unable to move for the rest of it. Some doctors feel that it is like being crushed to death from within. You are completely aware, but unable to move or communicate. You smile. For — what? — ten minutes. Half hour? You have a good imagination. Imagine that. Or. You could end a war.

REEVES. I'm not even sure this is a war. I think it's just — violence.

ARMY ATTORNEY. I may have underestimated you, Mr. Reeves.
(Then.)
There is a very narrow window for making this happen. I need your answer.
(No response.)
Mr. Reeves, you have antisocial personality disorder. Be aware of that. Don't let it destroy what hope there is.
(Then, Reeves at his best —)

REEVES. My squad. We were traffic cops. Our sergeant goes out to stop a car. Puts his hand out. Guy in the car shoots him. I don't know — the guy in the car — maybe he had antisocial personality disorder. What do you think? 'Cause I think — yeah, probably. Me? I stayed with my sergeant till the end. I looked in his eyes all the way. You can tell a lot from a person's eyes.

ARMY ATTORNEY. Yes, you can.

REEVES. Well, he never looked away from mine. I think he liked what he saw. I guess I wasn't feeling all that antisocial that day. And that was no fucking act.
(Army attorney respects that. Then —)

ARMY ATTORNEY. Did you tell the psychiatrist about that?

REEVES. You — you know about that?

ARMY ATTORNEY. Tell me about it.

REEVES. No. It's confidential.

ARMY ATTORNEY. Tell me.

REEVES. *(Duuuuuh?)*
It's *confidential.*

ARMY ATTORNEY. *(?, then — amused.)*
The confidentiality applies to the shrink. *He's* not supposed to tell what *you* say.

REEVES. *She* told me *I* couldn't tell what *she* said.

ARMY ATTORNEY. Mr. Reeves — I think we might have a case here.

(Then.)
Well, Mr. Reeves?
(A moment. Then —)
REEVES. You didn't tell me.
ARMY ATTORNEY. What?
REEVES. Is it worth it?
ARMY ATTORNEY. I just want to be the one to pose the question.
REEVES. You think — you think I might have the answer?
ARMY ATTORNEY. Who can tell? You might *be* the answer. Who can tell? The answer can be anything. A flag at Iwo Jima. A naked girl burning with napalm running down a highway. For this war — who knows?
REEVES. Maybe that little girl didn't want to be covered in napalm.
ARMY ATTORNEY. She's now a housewife with two children in Ontario, Canada. She ended a war.
REEVES. Would you have to say I did it?
ARMY ATTORNEY. I will say you did no more or no less than what you thought necessary to stay alive over there.
REEVES. I thought you didn't want the act.
ARMY ATTORNEY. I don't think that part of it is an act.
REEVES. No?
ARMY ATTORNEY. I believe in you, Mr. Reeves. It's as simple as that.
REEVES. I'm important?
ARMY ATTORNEY. Yes, Mr. Reeves. That is why I am here. There are two people in the world who think you are important. I'm the other one.
REEVES. All because I made the enemy feel pain?
ARMY ATTORNEY. Anyone can do that. You made them feel the pain of the enemy. That isn't the end of a war. That is the end of war. It is unendurable.
(Then.)
Did you feel it?
REEVES. The pain of the?
(A moment.)
There's a lot I don't feel. I got. I got this — disorder.
ARMY ATTORNEY. It's fairly common.
REEVES. Lot of people have it?
ARMY ATTORNEY. By my count, about 300 million. In your case, Mr. Reeves, you should be grateful. Very, very grateful.

31

REEVES. If I say yes ... will you be back?
(A moment, then —)
'Cause not that many people — talk with me.
ARMY ATTORNEY. *(Understood, then —)*
Is that a yes?
(It is.)
I will be back, Mr. Reeves.
(Before he goes —)
REEVES. Hey ... How long ago was the battle of Lepanto?
ARMY ATTORNEY. 1571.
REEVES. 1571? That *was* before my time.
ARMY ATTORNEY. Christendom versus the Ottoman Empire.
Our God versus theirs. Winner take all.
REEVES. Who won?
ARMY ATTORNEY. We did.
REEVES. Then how come we're still at war?
ARMY ATTORNEY. Maybe we were waiting for you.
(Army attorney exits — leaving behind his military hat.)
(Reeves tries to reclaim his best military self. His basic training. His military drills. He washes himself. When he is clean — the Pastor enters.)

CIRCLE 4 — FEDERAL PRISON

The pastor — folksy, with serious resolution under — carries a Bible.

Reeves waits for army attorney to come back. He's not coming back.

PASTOR. *(To audience.)* CIRCLE FOUR. FEDERAL PRISON.
SOME WEEKS LATER. BRINGING THE GOOD NEWS.
(The Pastor breaks the ice.)
Mornin'.
REEVES. Mornin'.
PASTOR. Nice day.

REEVES. I'll take your word for it. Can I help you?

PASTOR. Heard there was a soul that needs saving.

REEVES. I think you want cellblock D.

PASTOR. If you did what they *say* you did — son, you need Jesus.

REEVES. And if I didn't?

PASTOR. Well.

(Then —)

You still need Jesus.

REEVES. *(OK, then —)*

So it doesn't matter what I did. Well, *that's* a load off my mind.

PASTOR. I'm in over my head here, aren't I?

REEVES. You're just the wrong tool for the job. I don't need a pastor. I need a lawyer.

PASTOR. Son, the *last* thing you need is a lawyer.

REEVES. I talked to a lawyer. You look something like him.

PASTOR. I've got that kind of face.

REEVES. He said he'd come back.

PASTOR. Did he?

REEVES. Not yet. He made sense out of everything. Can't remember how.

PASTOR. He made it not your fault.

REEVES. How do you know that?

PASTOR. It's what lawyers do.

REEVES. Well, that's a good thing as far as I'm concerned.

PASTOR. *(Really?)*

Son, you raped a girl, led others to do the same and then you killed her and her whole family.

REEVES. You're sure I did that?

PASTOR. I am. Then you set fire to that girl's body and tried to put the blame on others. If you swore while you were doing it, you broke all ten of the Lord's commandments at one crack and broke 'em hard. Son, that *lawyer* was the wrong tool for the job. You need Jesus.

(A smile.)

And I'm going to take you to him.

(Reeves looks at the Pastor with anger. Thinks better of it. Smiles.)

REEVES. *(Self-containing.)*

I'm not going to get mad at you. I'm not going to shout. I'm not going to do that anymore. Fuck the act.

(Then, matter-of-fact.)

You want to talk about breaking commandments? You know what

they did to my friends after I left? They cut off their dicks, put them in their mouths, cut off their heads and then took pictures of themselves — laughing. That's what those people are like.

PASTOR. All of them?

REEVES. Close enough so it doesn't matter.

(Then.)

One day there was a kid — walking towards us. Couldn't have been more than eleven. Hot *hot* day and the kid is wearing an overcoat.

PASTOR. You shoot him?

REEVES. We don't do things like that. We got him to take off the coat.

PASTOR. You speak Arabic?

REEVES. Enough to make ourselves understood. And so he took off his coat, then his shirt, and there he was — in his underwear — covered in explosives. They strapped munitions onto an 11-year-old boy.

PASTOR. I never met an eleven-year-old boy didn't have munitions strapped to him ... I suspect you had more than most strapped on you.

REEVES. Look, why don't you go over there and bother them. If *anybody* needs Jesus, *they* do.

PASTOR. They aren't baptized. The minister from the base called me when he saw your picture in the papers. He told me he baptized you.

REEVES. Well, it didn't work.

PASTOR. Maybe he should have held you under longer.

REEVES. A few seconds more and it would've been waterboarding. Didn't work.

PASTOR. Worked on me. Made you my responsibility.

(Then.)

Speaking of lawyers. Your father hired a lawyer. It was in the paper.

REEVES. Really?

(With growing hope.)

Now why didn't anybody tell me that?

PASTOR. Why should they? The lawyer wasn't for you. He hired a lawyer to speak for him. Somebody he went to school with.

REEVES. *(Fuck it.)*

Wouldn't have done me any good anyway.

PASTOR. Not a good lawyer?

REEVES. Good enough if you're buying a house.

PASTOR. Son, I don't know who you have at this point but Jesus.

REEVES. *(Restraint failing.)*

Fuck Jesus. OK. *Fuck* Jesus. Where I was — the Tigris and Euphrates? — that's *Bible* land and there was no sign *anywhere* that *anybody* was one *bit better* for the *Bible* — and they had it *first,* OK?

(Then.)

No. I'm not going to shout.

PASTOR. *(I understand. In fact —)*

I was like you once. Didn't even believe Jesus lived. Till I read one verse. One verse changed my life.

REEVES. God is love?

PASTOR. *(No.)*

"Back off, you Syrian bitch."

(Silence. Then —)

REEVES. I don't recall ever hearing that one. And I had the book read to me when I was little.

PASTOR.

(Admittedly —)

It's a loose translation ... Woman comes up to Jesus. Says, "My daughter's dead. My little girl's dead. Can you bring her back to life?" And Jesus says to her, "Get away from me, you Syrian bitch."

(Then.)

At least, that's the sense of it.

REEVES. You are one fucked-up minister.

PASTOR. Actually, he says, "You don't give the master's meat to the dog under the table." Called her a dog. A female dog. It's in the book ... I expect that Arabs had been calling Jesus names for a long time and this Syrian woman asking him to perform a miracle for her — that was his limit.

REEVES. *(?)*

Out of ALL the verses in the Bible — ALL the miracles — all the HEALINGS — *that* saved you?

PASTOR. Who said I was saved? I'm a recovering alcoholic with an internet porn addiction I'm working on. Sometime I think I walk through life just exchanging one addiction for another. I'm a weak and shallow vessel but I believe in Christ Jesus the Lord.

REEVES. Because he said, "Back off, you fucking Syrian bitch?"

PASTOR. See, the thing is — nobody would put words like that into the mouth of their Savior and Lord. Would they?

(Then.)
I mean who would dare add his own darkness to the Savior's blinding light. *Nobody* would make that up. Nobody could.

REEVES. Guess not.

PASTOR. *(Exactly.)*
He had to be *real* to say that. And if he was real, why — there is hope for us all.

REEVES. You know, you're the first pastor I ever met I might be able to talk to … Maybe we should go back and start over with our area of common interest.

PASTOR. And what is that?

REEVES. Internet porn.

PASTOR. Son, read the book and prepare yourself for the shit-storm that is about to hit you. There is a fair amount of shit repellent in here. It'll help when the storm comes your way.

(Reeves takes the Bible. Then —)

REEVES. The girl — she wasn't dead.

PASTOR. The paper said you shot her dead.

REEVES. No, not her. The Syrian girl. In the story. I know that story. She wasn't dead.

PASTOR. No — matter of fact — she wasn't.

REEVES. Girl in the story was possessed by a demon. The mother asked Jesus to drive the demon out. You changed that part of the story.

PASTOR. Yes, I did. Out of respect for you.

REEVES. You think I'm possessed, Pastor?

PASTOR. It would be a comfort to me to think you were. Otherwise — we're just talking about plain I-don't-give-a-fuck human evil and even God himself is helpless before that. Are you?

REEVES. Am I what?

PASTOR. *(Taking courage to ask —)*
Are you evil, son?

REEVES. *(Amused.)*
Well, I'm not possessed. No voices in here. No distractions and 20-10 vision. I think I could have been a sniper.

(His head.)
It's quiet in here. Lonely sometimes. Might be good to have a voice or two to talk to.

PASTOR. Voices in your head aren't interested in conversation. I knew a young man killed himself.

REEVES. Voices?

PASTOR. *(Yes.)*
There was some discussion as to whether he should be buried in consecrated ground or not.
REEVES. Well?
PASTOR. What?
REEVES. Was he? Buried in consecrated ground?
PASTOR. Do funerals interest you, son? ... Maybe that's where I should've started. Maybe that's our area of common interest. Paper says you came here to see a funeral.
REEVES. I don't want to talk about that.
PASTOR. *(Understanding.)*
Because those three men who just got buried — they died for you.
REEVES. Well, that's a funny way to put it, but I believe — had I been there — they'd still be alive. I.
(Then —)
I don't want to talk about them.
PASTOR. Would you care to talk about the rape?
REEVES. It's the rape that interests you, isn't it?
PASTOR. It doesn't bother me unduly. Tell you the truth, I'm not sure I believe in consensual sex. I mean somebody always wants it more, right? It's rare that need and desire are equally matched.
REEVES. You are the god-damnest minister.
PASTOR. I suspect I am.
REEVES. You're enjoying this, aren't you?
PASTOR. Tell the truth, you scare the shit out of me. I'm scared to be here with you. Scared to say what I have to say. Still, it's my duty to bring you to the Lord. Even at the end.
(Then, with new seriousness —)
REEVES. I don't want a funeral. When I'm dead, leave my body on a couch in a vacant lot. Let dogs come and eat it. I'd like that.
PASTOR. Really?
REEVES. *(No, then — for real.)*
I'd like to get shot and go out on a hummer hood.
PASTOR. You don't have to punish yourself, son. God will do that for you.
(Reeves appreciates this. Amused —)
REEVES. He already has.
PASTOR. Yes, he has. More than you know.
(A moment —)
REEVES. What don't I know?

(No response.)
What?
PASTOR. *(A risk.)*
They're saying now — it was done for revenge.
REEVES. Really?
(Reeves laughs.)
Well, that's a relief. I knew somebody would figure that out. See, we all figured some hajjis — they killed the girl for revenge. Maybe an honor killing. That's what they do over there. Nothing but revenge.
PASTOR. I wasn't talking about the girl.
REEVES. Who then?
(Very careful. Very delicate.)
PASTOR. Your friends. The soldiers. The ones just got buried. They're saying now that *they* were killed for revenge.
REEVES. Revenge? For what?
(No response.)
What?
PASTOR. For the rape of a young girl.
(Silence. Then, Reeves laughs with relief.)
REEVES. Now that just shows your ignorance. They would never have anything to do with something like that.
(The Pastor lays this out carefully.)
PASTOR. Maybe it didn't matter.
(Then, feeling at risk.)
Maybe the family of the girl wanted revenge.
(Then.)
That's how they are, after all. According to you.
(Then.)
Maybe they saw your friends, your brothers — three American soldiers in a Hummer — unprotected. They weren't the soldiers they wanted — they *wanted* you — they wanted the man who raped their child — but maybe any Americans were close enough so it didn't matter.
(Then — getting what the Pastor is laying out —)
REEVES. Are you saying — ?
PASTOR. I am.
REEVES. Are you saying it was because of *me* they got killed?
PASTOR. If you killed that family. Did you, son?
REEVES. No.
(Then, attacking him.)
And you're a sick fuck to make that up.

PASTOR. But I didn't make it up.

REEVES. Where'd you get it then?

PASTOR. Internet.

REEVES. You know, there's a lot of bullshit on the internet.

PASTOR. True enough, but I believe this.

REEVES. Yeah? Why?

PASTOR. Because it's like that story.

REEVES. Which?

PASTOR. Of the Syrian woman.

(Then.)

It's one of those stories you just couldn't make up.

(Then.)

Don't think anybody could.

(The implications begin to shake Reeves.)

They were killed for you, son. They died for your sins. Somebody had to and you wouldn't let Jesus do it for you.

REEVES. I don't believe it.

PASTOR. I didn't either. At first. But it makes sense, doesn't it, when you think about it. I mean, the violence of their deaths — that feels *personal.* The kind of thing oh a father might do —

REEVES. I want a lawyer.

PASTOR. *(Pleased.)*

Wrong tool for the job.

REEVES. They did *not* die for me.

PASTOR. The thing that worries me is — what were they thinking as they were dying — your friends. Did they think they were dying for their country?

REEVES. They had their parade. Nothing can hurt them now.

PASTOR. Or did one of the Iraqis know enough English to make it clear what they were dying for? Did somebody make it understood to them that they were dying for you. For Daniel Reeves and his demons.

REEVES. *(Deep denial.)*

You'll say anything — anything at all — to get me to come to Jesus.

PASTOR. Have I disturbed the quiet of your mind?

REEVES. Is that what you wanted?

PASTOR. Yes, I believe so.

REEVES. Jesus drove demons out. He didn't drive them *in.*

PASTOR. No, he didn't. But there's no confusing me with Jesus, is there?

(Then.)
Well, I'll be going now. I'll just leave the Bible in case you want to take a look. I've marked that story.

REEVES. You want voices — you want voices telling me to kill myself like that boy in your story, don't you?

PASTOR. Oh, the voices didn't tell him to kill himself.

REEVES. No?

PASTOR. The voices told him to kill his family … That's why he killed himself. So when they asked if that boy should be buried in consecrated ground, I said there was no worry there. Wherever that boy was buried would be consecrated ground. He was a hero in death. And that's what I want for you, boy. Same thing you want for yourself. You want to be a hero, don't you, boy?

REEVES. Man, why are you doing this?

PASTOR. *(Truth.)*
The girl.

REEVES. I thought that didn't bother you.

PASTOR. Not so much the rape, terrible as that is.

REEVES. What then?

PASTOR. The fire. You set fire to her body. See, that's where your sin comes face to face with my addiction. I can't stand to see beauty vandalized.

REEVES. *(Powerful truth.)*
I didn't do that.

PASTOR. Don't deny it, son.

REEVES. *(Very strong and sure.)*
I told them not to. I — didn't — do — that.
(A moment. Then —)

PASTOR. No, you probably didn't. The man who did that was ashamed of what he did … But you did the rest, didn't you, son?
(Reeves grows increasingly agitated as the Pastor prepares to leave.)
Don't lose heart, son. Let it be a call. Even Jesus needed a call. The woman said to him, "Maybe I don't get the meat from your table, but even dogs can have a crust of bread." And he threw her a crust. He drove out the demon. There is hope. For us all.
(Pastor exits. Reeves takes the Bible that has been left and as guards put Reeves into restrains — wrists and ankles — in a chair that is bolted to the floor — Reeves first reads and then recites the passage from the Bible that the pastor told him about.)

REEVES. *(As he is bound, increasingly wild, from the Bible.)*

For a certain woman, whose young daughter had an unclean spirit, heard of him, and came and fell at his feet: The woman was a Greek, a Syrophenician by nation; and she besought him that he would cast forth the devil out of her daughter. But Jesus said unto her, Let the children first be filled: for it is not meet to take the children's bread, and to cast it unto the dogs. (Back off you fucking Syrian bitch!) And she answered and said unto him, Yes, Lord: yet the dogs under the table eat of the children's crumbs. And he said unto her, For this saying go thy way; the devil is gone out of thy daughter. And when he was come to her house, she found the devil gone out, and her daughter laid upon the bed. Let the children first be filled: for it is not meet to take the children's bread, and to cast it unto the dogs. Let the children first be filled: for it is not meet to take the children's bread, and to cast it unto the dogs. *(A civilian lawyer enters.)*

CIRCLE 5 — TELL ME ABOUT THE DOG

Civilian lawyer. 40s. Smart. Professional. Disheveled. Definitely not military. His full is attention on Reeves, even when it does not seem to be.

Reeves — fierce military bearing over self-hate and exhaustion. Reeves's eyes are fixed. Unblinking. Reeves is in restraints throughout.

WOMAN. CIRCLE FIVE — SOME WEEKS LATER. TELL ME ABOUT THE DOG.
LAWYER. Mr. Reeves. I will be representing you in your trial.
(No response.)
They did tell you I was coming, didn't they?
REEVES. *(Hyper-military gung ho.)*
SIR, YES, SIR.
(The lawyer is taken aback by this. Then —)
LAWYER. Before you entered the army, you went through several trials, didn't you, Mr. Reeves, for some petty crimes?

REEVES. SIR, YES, SIR!

LAWYER. Mr. Reeves —

REEVES. SIR?

LAWYER. Mr. Reeves, we're going to be having *many* conversations and a great deal is going to have to be accomplished in a *limited* amount of time. I suspect our work will be *more* productive if we could lower the volume.

REEVES. SIR, I DOUBT THAT, SIR.

LAWYER. That quieter might be more productive?

REEVES. THAT WE'LL BE HAVING MANY CONVERSATIONS.

LAWYER. Go on.

REEVES. PEOPLE SEEM TO SPEAK TO ME ONCE AND THEN NEVER RETURN, SIR.

LAWYER. OK. Say this is the only conversation we are ever going to have. Say that when I leave this room I am hit by a beer truck and die. It would *still* be easier on me if we could make the tone a little more civil. A little more — *civilian.*

REEVES. *Sir,* yes, *sir!*

LAWYER. Mr. Reeves, you know you're not in the military, don't you?

REEVES. You don't have to be in the army to talk this way, *sir.*

LAWYER. But if you aren't, why would you?

REEVES. To get off the medication they have me on, I have to be on an emotional even keel. Talking this way helps, sir. I've been through trials in civilian life, sir. Three. Drugs, alcohol, fights.

LAWYER. But you've always pled guilty, so you've only ever seen *half* a trial. In a trial a story is told twice. In the first version you are guilty. In the second — same story — you are innocent.

REEVES. SIR, I'm guilty, SIR.

LAWYER. Doesn't matter. At least not to me.

REEVES. Sir — if I'm being tried for a crime I'm guilty of — shouldn't it *especially* matter to you?

LAWYER. There's a jury to decide that. I have one job. And that job is to defend you. Do you know what that means?

REEVES. Proving I didn't do what I did. I'm not going to let that happen, SIR. I'm guilty, SIR.

LAWYER. What's harder these days, Daniel? Not eating or not sleeping?

REEVES. *Cramps,* sir. I can't *shit,* sir. It's the medication. I killed the hajjis, sir. We went to their shack and I killed them. I'm *guilty.*

LAWYER. *(A moment, then —)*
Prove it.
REEVES. Sir?
LAWYER. Prove it.
REEVES. I was *there,* sir. I *know* what I *did.*
LAWYER. Mr. Reeves, if I wanted to know what you did, you would be the *last* person I would ask. We know very little of ourselves.
REEVES. Maybe you don't know *your*self, sir.
LAWYER. The one thing I am certain of is that we are not who we think we are.
REEVES. SIR, I was warned about you. You'll turn everything upside down. You're a lawyer, SIR.
LAWYER. Who warned you about lawyers?
REEVES. A preacher, sir.
LAWYER. Preachers usually turn things upside down. Did he? *(A nod.)*
Well, then, I'm just putting things back.
REEVES. *(Fighting going mad.)*
Don't play with me, sir. People always play with me. They say they'll come back and they don't. They say, "Say 'not guilty'" then they throw me in jail. They swear me in and then throw me out. I think it's driving me insane. SIR.
LAWYER. Mr. Reeves — I'll plead you guilty.
REEVES. Thank you, sir.
LAWYER. — if you will just give me one shred of evidence that you were involved in a crime.
REEVES. Like what?
LAWYER. Spent cartridges, semen stains, blood samples, a murder weapon. A dead body would help.
REEVES. SIR, you may not have NOTICED, SIR, but I am in RESTRAINTS in a CELL in a FEDERAL PRISON. Where am I going to get any of that *SHIT?*
LAWYER. Where is *anybody* going to get any of that shit? That's what I'd like to know. There is no case — at least not in the conventional sense — against you.
REEVES. I'm *guilty,* sir.
LAWYER. *(OK, then —)*
There is one thing I think I *can* prove you guilty of.
REEVES. Sir?
LAWYER. There was an incident with a dog.

REEVES. A dog?

LAWYER. You threw a dog off a roof?

REEVES. Fuck the dog, sir.

LAWYER. A surprising number of people *saw* you do that. If you want to be guilty of something, I suspect I can prove you guilty of that.

REEVES. *Fuck* the dog.

LAWYER. The dog —

REEVES. *Fuck the dog!*

LAWYER. OK, if it upsets you. Let's — Let's talk about the girl you killed.

REEVES. *(Easy with that.)*

Alright.

(Puzzled by Reeves' lack of upset —)

LAWYER. It doesn't bother you to talk about her?

REEVES. Sir, no, sir! I don't give a fuck about the girl.

LAWYER. That surprises me. I thought that's what you were guilty of.

(Preempting.)

I'm not playing with you. This is the crime. What happened with the girl. That's what this trial is about. What you demand to be guilty for. And yet you don't feel bad about her?

REEVES. She ruined a lot of good men's lives, sir.

LAWYER. *She* did.

REEVES. By her, I mean all of them in their fucked up-country, sir. She fucked up a lot of good men's lives.

LAWYER. She was fourteen.

REEVES. She doesn't *matter*. She really doesn't *matter*.

LAWYER. Well, if she doesn't, who does? Who are you so anxious to give up your life for?

REEVES. *(Looking him over, then —)*

You were never in the military, were you, sir?

(No.)

Then you wouldn't understand.

LAWYER. The brotherhood. The camaraderie.

REEVES. *(His deepest belief.)*

Sir, yes, sir.

LAWYER. You feel bad for the men you left behind. The ones who were beheaded and mutilated — because of what you did to the girl.

(Reeves can scarcely bear hearing this. He struggles against his restraints.)

Mr. Reeves — *they* don't matter.

REEVES. *The fuck they don't.*

LAWYER. You are not being tried for their deaths.

REEVES. *(Violent bottom line.)*

I'm guilty. I will tell them I'm guilty!

LAWYER. *(Violent bottom line.)*

I will *not* let you testify *against yourself.* Not in *court.* Not in *here.*

(Finger on Reeves' forehead.)

And not in *here.*

(A long moment of contact. Reeves takes that in. Lawyer removes his finger.)

REEVES. *(Simple and sad.)*

I did it, sir. I'm guilty.

LAWYER. One remarkable thing about a trial is — even if a person is guilty, if his story can be presented in such a way as to make the *reason* for his actions comprehensible — no matter how strange they might seem in the cold light of day — if they can be shown to have made sense at the time to the person doing them — people tend to understand.

(Then.)

I think that's wonderful.

REEVES. A sympathetic reaction.

LAWYER. Yes, exactly.

REEVES. I've had them, sir. Twice.

LAWYER. Just twice?

REEVES. Sir, I think that's more than most.

LAWYER. Well, we only need *one.* One member of the jury who understands your story. But to tell the story in that way — I will have to know who you are — exactly who you are — in the story — what you did — why you did it.

(Then.)

Now, would you like people to understand what you did?

REEVES. I'd like to understand it myself.

LAWYER. Just answer my questions, OK?

(A nod, then, seriously.)

Tell me about the dog.

REEVES. *(Instantaneous.)*

Fuck the *dog.*

LAWYER. Why did you throw the dog off the roof?

REEVES. *Fuck! The Dog!*

LAWYER. *You want to be guilty about something? Start here.* You

DID this. Why? *Why did you throw the dog off the roof?*
REEVES. I thought it was —
(What?)
— funny.
LAWYER. Funny. Funny? Killing a dog? Did other people find it —
REEVES. Other people *freaked.* That's funny, right?
LAWYER. Not to the dog.
REEVES. Really? You know what a dog thinks? *You* do? You can *prove* the dog *didn't* think it was funny? Who knows — maybe the dog thought it was funny. Dogs think *everything* is funny. Maybe the dog thought it could *fly* — *what* the *fuck* are we *talking* about? Look, am I being charged with *cruelty to animals?*
LAWYER. You and your buddies are being charged with rape and murder. Capital crimes.
REEVES. How are they pleading?
LAWYER. Guilty.
REEVES. How come they get to plead guilty and I don't?
LAWYER.   Because they got a deal. Plead guilty and live.
REEVES. Get me the same deal.
LAWYER. I can't.
REEVES. Then get me a new lawyer.
LAWYER. It doesn't have to do with me. You can't do what they're doing.
REEVES. What?
LAWYER. They're testifying against you, Daniel. They are *lining up* to testify — they are *falling over themselves* to testify against you. They're going to nail your hide to the barn door, Mr. Reeves, your brothers-in-arms. See, they know who *they* are in the story. They're the ones who are out on parole in ten years — all because they are willing to throw you off the roof, Daniel.
(Reeves struggles with his restraints —)
It doesn't have to be that way.
(Then.)
All they have are fifteen photographs of the crime scene. That's *all* they have and those photographs were used as proof that the killings were the work of insurgents. *Everyone* up-and-down the line signed on to that. Fifteen photos and the testimony of your squadmates — every single one of whom is seriously and repeatedly *perjured.* They've got *nothing.* There is no evidence against you.
REEVES. You want evidence against me — dig up the girl.

46

LAWYER. Daniel —
REEVES. *Dig up the girl.*
LAWYER.
(With sudden edge.)
Please don't talk about "the girl." She has a name. Hayat. It means
"life."
(Sensing his sympathy for the girl —)
REEVES. You know I'm guilty. Don't you?
LAWYER. I am trying to understand what happened *inside* you.
REEVES. I don't know.
LAWYER. OK. Let's figure it out. You walk into the room and
you see the girl being held down on the floor. Was she struggling?
Was she crying?
REEVES. Crying. Screaming. It was embarrassing.
LAWYER. Why were you embarrassed? What did she scream?
REEVES. She said "Sa'idny."
LAWYER. "Sa'idny"? What does "Sa'idny" mean?
REEVES. I don't know.
LAWYER. You know some Arabic. You talked to the locals in it.
What did she —
REEVES. I don't know. "Fuck you, Americans."
LAWYER. *(Driving.)*
I don't think so. You would have understood that. What does
"Sa'idny" mean?
REEVES. *How am I supposed to know?*
LAWYER. Well, what did you *feel*? *That's* the important thing —
REEVES. I have a personality disorder. I don't feel things.
LAWYER. Of course you do.
REEVES. *I DON'T FEEL —*
LAWYER. Mr. Reeves, you feel so many things, they had to
restrain you. You are pumped full of pharmaceuticals just to keep
you functioning. You walked into a room and saw a girl struggling.
Two people, your brothers, are holding her down. A lovely four-
teen-year-old girl. You look at her and you felt —
REEVES. *Nothing.*
LAWYER. Did you think it was funny?
REEVES. Are you sick?
LAWYER. You thought killing the dog was funny.
REEVES. Killing the dog wasn't the funny part.
LAWYER. What was?

REEVES. FUCK THE DOG! IF YOU WANT PROOF AGAINST ME — DIG — HER — UP.

LAWYER. Even if Islamic law allowed it, I don't think it would prove anything.

REEVES. I WAS THERE. What happened *happened*. We *raped* and *killed* a girl.

LAWYER. Prove it.

(Then.)

Source of Information 3 isn't sure about what he did. He says he attempted to rape the girl but —

(His notes.)

— *"he was not sure if he had done so."*

(Then.)

SOI2 says the same. I am not saying this wasn't horrific, but I do *not* think it is what it seems to be. What happened? Are you *sure* you raped that girl?

REEVES. *(Enough of this.)*

I'm sure I killed the bitch.

LAWYER. *(Enough of this.)*

But then again —

(The heart of the matter.)

You're also sure you caused the deaths of three men at a checkpoint.

REEVES. SIR, YES, SIR.

LAWYER. Prove it.

REEVES. Huh?

LAWYER. Prove — it. Prove one event had any connection whatsoever with the other.

(Then.)

That's what you really feel guilty for? That's what you want to die for — not the girl? OK, I get that. Just *prove* it.

REEVES. *(Baffled.)*

Sir?

LAWYER. At the time they — your buddies — at the time they were killed, when their bodies were put on display — when the videos were made and shown? Nobody said a word — not a word — about the girl or her family. The story didn't come out for *weeks*. Then Al Jazeera combined the two stories and created a propaganda bonanza. Why would they sit on a story that was *that* good if there was *any* truth to it *at all?* People believe it because it is a *terrific* story.

(Then.)

You believe it because it flatters your ego. It makes you important — tragic even. It gives you something easy to confess to.

REEVES. Easy? EASY?

LAWYER. It's always easy to be guilty of something you *didn't* do. It makes *you* the victim instead of the girl — but there is *no proof* the events are *related*. I do *not* believe that they are or we would have heard about it the *instant* it happened.

REEVES. Are you lying to me?

LAWYER. I'm a lawyer, Mr. Reeves. That is an awkward question.

REEVES. DO NOT PLAY WITH ME.

LAWYER. The good news is — I do *not* think you are responsible for the deaths of your squad mates at the checkpoint. The bad news is your other squad mates are shopping you for reduced sentences. The simple *truth* is you are what you have always been — an individual human being with a story to tell. Now tell it to me. There is nothing to hide. Tell me, Daniel. You walk in and you see her on the floor, you look in her eyes —

REEVES. They're testifying against me?

LAWYER. Yes, Daniel. I am sorry, but they are.

REEVES. *(With growing anger.)*
I am not the dog.

LAWYER. Good.

REEVES. I am NOT the dog! I AM NOT —

LAWYER. Tell me about the dog.

REEVES. We were up to our asses in *dead bodies*. We were wearing *full body armor,* carrying *automatic weapons* walking around looking for *people* to kill and everybody went *nuts* when I threw a *dog* off a *roof.*
(Amused.)
"He killed the dog! There's something wrong with him — he killed the dog."
(Then, laughing.)
The *dog.*

LAWYER. Go on.

REEVES. And it's *funny.* I mean, all this shit is going on — bombings and body parts — and they point at *me* and say, "Look at *that!* What *he* did? *That's* wrong. He killed a *dog.*" *It's funny.* But it's not. Is it? I mean, not to the dog. You think I'm the *dog* off the *roof* AND IT'S NOT — FUCKING — FUNNY!

LAWYER. Daniel, please believe I never thought that. You are not the dog.

REEVES. Who am I then?

LAWYER. *(With growing enthusiasm.)*

That's the other thing I can prove. I can *prove* that you are the person — the *only* person in this whole affair who said, "Something is wrong here." You are the *only* one who sought help — *before* the event — to get out of this mess. You sought help and they said — well, we don't know what they said because the psychiatrist you went to won't say *what* she said. She won't testify.

REEVES. She won't?

LAWYER. Not without a grant of immunity.

REEVES. What does that mean?

LAWYER. *(Driving forward.)*

It means she thinks she did something very wrong. Something that she *does* — *not* — *want* on the record. But you went on the record. In a culture in which seeking help is the *last* thing you do, you sought help. And I need to know what went on in that conversation. What did she say?

REEVES. It's confidential.

LAWYER. What did she say that was so terrible?

REEVES. It's confidential.

LAWYER. I need to know, Daniel, or there is no second story to tell at your trial.

REEVES. Dig her up. I'm guilty. DIG — HER — UP.

LAWYER. There would be no point, Daniel. She's dead. Her family is dead. All that's left of that girl is in here. All that's left of this whole incident is in here.

(Daniel's head.)

REEVES. *(Wild.)*

I — AM — THE — DOG. I — AM — THE — DOG.

LAWYER. What did you tell the shrink, Daniel?

REEVES. *(Wilder.)*

I TOLD HER I WANTED TO KILL EVERYBODY.

LAWYER. And what did she say?

REEVES. *(Wildest.)*

SHE SAID I WAS NORMAL!

(Immediately —)

SHRINK. *(Immediately, mid-scene.)*

Well, do you want to kill *me*?

CIRCLE 6: SYMPATHETIC REACTION

Reeves — in uniform — three months before all the shit hits — faces the Shrink — also in uniform.

She's tired of dealing with inarticulate nineteen-year-olds. Most of what she does is push paper and dispense medication. Given a chance, she'd do more.

Reeves tries to contain himself, but inside he is a horse in a burning barn — incapable of the move he must make.

REEVES. No. I don't want to kill you.
SHRINK. So you don't want to kill *everybody?*
(Then.)
Go on. What's on your mind?
MAN. CIRCLE SIX. IRAQ. A YEAR EARLIER.
(The man places a bottle of prescription pills on the stage before leaving.)
REEVES. I say I want to kill everybody. You tell me I don't. What is there to talk about?
SHRINK. Are you trying to get out of the service?
REEVES. *No, ma'am.*
(No response. Then, too casual —)
Man, a shrink in the army — that's just — crazy.
SHRINK. This isn't about me.
REEVES. *(Immediate and* not *casual.)*
Well, I'm not ready for it to be about me.
SHRINK. Have you ever seen a shrink before?
REEVES. School counselor. Social worker. Parole officer. I know the drill. Aren't you supposed to ask me some questions?
SHRINK. You want me to ask you some questions?
REEVES. Whatever.
SHRINK. *(From a form/almost by heart.)*
Have you experienced a traumatic event where your or someone else's life was in danger or you thought that your or someone else's life was in danger?
REEVES. You're joking, right?

SHRINK. *(Sort of.)*
How did you react to the trauma?
REEVES. *(Enjoying this.)*
You got some choices there?
SHRINK. *(The form.)*
Were you frightened or horrified? While it was happening did it seem like things were unreal, like a dream?
(No response.)
Did it seem like your body or some part of your body was somehow changed, not real, or detached from you?
REEVES. No, but if a body part does become detached, I'll come back and discuss it with you.
(Reeves starts out.)
SHRINK. One word, private. Give me one word and I'll do my best.
(Preempting.)
Not "whatever."
REEVES. "Whatever" covers a lot of territory.
SHRINK. You're a smart guy. You ought to be able to come up with one word.
REEVES. What makes you think I'm smart?
SHRINK. You're here. And nobody made you come and you're here.
(No response.)
Private, everything that happens here is confidential.
(Reeves laughs.)
You don't believe that.
REEVES. Never had a confidential conversation that what I said wasn't public knowledge before I got home. You'll tell *somebody.*
SHRINK. And you'll go back to barracks and tell everybody how we did it on the desk until the desk broke and we still kept doing it and you've got another appointment not because you need it but because I do.
(Silence. Then — Reeves laughs. She sees an opening. What the hell. Takes it.)
A shrink in the army. It's crazy. Crazy I'm here, crazy you're here, the whole thing is crazy.
REEVES. Not so crazy — defending our country.
SHRINK. You think?
REEVES. You don't?
(Easy back-and-forth. A dance.)
SHRINK. Doesn't matter what I think.

REEVES. Matters to me. I need to talk. I need to know I can trust who I'm talking to. I tell you I want to kill everybody and you tell me I don't. I think that's fucked up.

SHRINK. What do you want me to say?

REEVES. Maybe you should say what you think?

SHRINK. Doesn't matter what I think.

REEVES. Matters if you want to hear what I'm thinking.

(A moment. Then —)

SHRINK. I think maybe wanting to kill everybody is a deviation from the norm in Texas — maybe — but over here — under the circumstances — very unofficially — yeah — that's pretty normal. Is that what you wanted to know — if you're normal?

REEVES. You tell me wanting to kill everybody is normal. Makes me wonder what kind of a home you came from. I think you're a fucked-up shrink in this fucked-up war. I'd like to know what you think of that.

(A test?)

SHRINK. Confidential?

REEVES. Confidential.

(A nod from Reeves.)

SHRINK. I don't think this is a war.

REEVES. No?

SHRINK. I think this is just — violence.

REEVES. Wars are violence.

SHRINK. Violence *for* something.

REEVES. This *isn't* for something?

SHRINK. What do you *think?*

REEVES. What do *you* think?

SHRINK. I think this is just a mistake.

REEVES. A mistake?

SHRINK. We invaded the wrong country and — ever since — everything's fucked up. And the puzzle is — once we knew it was the wrong place, why we didn't pull out. That's what I think of this fucked-up war.

(Reeves is lost in his own thoughts.)

That was my best shot at honest. Your turn.

(Silence.)

OK, you come back when you're ready. We're done here.

REEVES. So — you think he was an idiot, right?

SHRINK. Who?

REEVES. The sergeant.

SHRINK. What sergeant?

REEVES. Ortiz.

(With new seriousness —)

SHRINK. Why would he be an idiot?

REEVES. 'Cause he thought he was over here fighting for his country. But this is all just a big mistake, right? That's what you think.

SHRINK. Were you there?

(He was.)

REEVES. He died under me.

SHRINK. He was the sergeant. You were under him.

REEVES. They grabbed Sgt. Ortiz. Tossed him on the Hummer hood. I jumped on him. Don't know why. Held him on the hood all the way back to base. We were going fast, but I never looked where we were going. I just looked at him and held him on the hood. I was on top of him. All the way. On the hood. He died *under* me.

(A moment. Then —)

SHRINK. Soldier, just to clarify, I don't think the sergeant was an idiot for being here.

REEVES. *(Instantaneous painful reversal.)*

He was an idiot. He had no business being here. Fighting for his country, shit. It wasn't even his country. He wasn't even a citizen.

SHRINK. He was what — an alien?

REEVES. An — an *alien?*

SHRINK. Resident alien?

REEVES. Ma'am?

SHRINK. "Resident alien." It's an oxymoron? "Non-dairy creamer?" Something that means its own opposite.

REEVES. Ma'am, I don't have a clue what you're talking about.

(Rising to go.)

Well, this has been *very* therapeutic, but I think that maybe I came to the wrong place — like we invaded the wrong country — so maybe I should just leave like we should have.

SHRINK. Sit down, private.

REEVES. No, ma'am.

SHRINK. You afraid of talking to me, private?

REEVES. No, ma'am.

SHRINK. Then what are you afraid of?

REEVES. *I'm afraid of killing everybody, ma'am. But you don't want to hear me say that, ma'am. You're* afraid *to hear me say that. That's what* you're *afraid of.*

SHRINK. How about Sgt. Ortiz? What would he do if you told him you wanted to kill everybody?

REEVES. He'd do what he always did. He'd put his hand out with a big smile. Like at the roadblock. He walked up to the car like he walked up to everybody. Even in cammies and Kevlar, that's all you could see when he came up to you. A smile and his hand out. He had his daughter's name tattooed on his wrist so you could see that too. The guy in the car smiled back at him. Put his hand out. There was a gun in it. He shot him. Just like that. He shot Timmons too. Timmons fell down dead.

(Silence.)

Sgt. Ortiz was alive. Most of the way. Looking at me. He never looked away. I never looked away from him. Never once.

(He holds his look at her for a while. Then can't.)

SHRINK. Did he say anything?

REEVES. No, ma'am. He was dignified. Never complained. Not a word.

SHRINK. Did you say anything?

REEVES. Oh, yeah. I was real poetic.

SHRINK. What did you say?

REEVES. I said "Sgt. Ortiz. Sgt. Ortiz." See, I got a way with words. "Sgt. Ortiz."

(Then.)

Fucking stupid thing to say.

SHRINK. That was his name.

REEVES. *(Fuck you.)*

That was his *job.* His *name* was Rudy. At least I could of said Rudy. He was fucking dying. You think you'd say his name.

SHRINK. Anything else?

REEVES. No, ma'am.

(Silence. A thought. Dismissed.)

SHRINK. What?

REEVES. Well —

SHRINK. What?

REEVES. I drooled on him. Pretty great, huh? I wiped it off.

(Then.)

Like it mattered.

(Then.)

He wouldn't care about a little spit.

SHRINK. It mattered to you.

REEVES. He was *dying.* And here I am — *drooling* on him. I could have —

SHRINK. What?

REEVES. He liked jokes. He told jokes. How do you know you've been in Iraq too long? Ask me. Go on. Ask me.

SHRINK. How do you know you've been in Iraq too long?

REEVES. You know all the lines in the fourth season of *Sex in the City.*

(He nods for her to ask again.)

SHRINK. How do you know you've been in Iraq too long?

REEVES. You start thinking of building a house for your family someplace nice — like the Green Zone.

(Reeves laughs.)

SHRINK. How do you know you've been in Iraq too long?

REEVES. *(Laughing.)*

You're in the Army and you start saying Ooorah … Or in the Marines and you start saying Hooah. Or the temperature drops to 102 degrees and you put on a jacket.

(Silence.)

(Reeves is about to cry.)

SHRINK. You didn't tell him a joke.

(Silence.)

REEVES. I rubbed his chest. I said "Sgt. Ortiz." He died. And that's the trauma, right?

SHRINK. If it bothered you, it is.

REEVES. If it *didn't* bother me, it is too, right?

SHRINK. You're a smart guy.

REEVES. Nothing smart about it. It's a trick. You just say the opposite of what people say to you — it confuses them.

SHRINK. Why are you letting me in on the trick?

REEVES. I suppose one of us shouldn't be confused.

SHRINK. Are you confused about what happened?

REEVES. No, ma'am, I am not. It did *not* seem like a dream. I did not leave my body.

(Amused.)

He left his though.

(Not amused.)

He surely did.

(Then, with hard, sincere compassion —)
SHRINK. I think you did a very hard thing. I think you accompanied a man to his death. I think you called his name to make sure that he knew he wasn't alone. You touched him with gentleness. You eased his passing. I think you did a great thing. I think he did a great thing being the kind of man you could look up to. Maybe that's what this is all about. Maybe that's why we came here. For that to happen.
(Then, with extreme, *focused anger —)*
REEVES. That's the *most* fucked-up thing I've ever heard.
(Silence.)
SHRINK. Tell me about it.
(Then — with violent anger —)
REEVES. No, ma'am. I got *nothing* to say to somebody who thinks this war is about letting Sgt. Ortiz die so I can see it. I think that is fucked up.
SHRINK. You mad?
(No response.)
How mad?
REEVES. Ask me *now* if I'd like to kill you.
SHRINK. *(Hard ass.)*
Private Reeves, you say you want to stay in the service?
REEVES. YES, MA'AM.
SHRINK. Well, there are certain things I *cannot* hear. If you tell me you want to kill everybody or kill yourself, I have to warehouse you. If you *don't* want to go home, do NOT tell me that you want to commit MURDER or SUICIDE.
REEVES. Then it seems to me that there's AN EXTREMELY LIMITED RANGE of things that are OPEN for DISCUSSION.
(Silence. Then — hard, fast, diagnostic —)
SHRINK. If a bullet came through the tent and I were bleeding here on the floor, would that bother you?
REEVES. No, ma'am. Would it bother you if that happened to me?
SHRINK. Yes, it would.
REEVES. Why?
SHRINK. You see somebody die, it's disturbing.
REEVES. Why?
SHRINK. It's a sympathetic reaction. You forget it's happening to somebody else. It feels like it's happening to you.
REEVES. Does it, ma'am? You're sure of that.

SHRINK. *(Yes.)*

It's an emotional thing. It confuses the brain. It's what makes us human. Even in a movie. You have a sympathetic response. Watching a football game, you take sides — you feel you win when your team wins.

REEVES. I've never been much of a team player, ma'am.

SHRINK. You were on Sgt. Ortiz's team.

REEVES. Yes, ma'am.

SHRINK. Did his death bother you?

REEVES. No, ma'am.

SHRINK. What did?

REEVES. That I didn't *kill* the *fuck* who *shot* him *before* he had the chance.

SHRINK. Soldier, you couldn't have saved him.

REEVES. No?

SHRINK. The way you tell it, not enough time to aim and fire.

REEVES. *(Sure there was.)*

If I had him in my sights.

SHRINK. You going to keep them all in your sights all of the time?

REEVES. You think we're not in their sights all the time? Could of shot him as soon as he got out of the car. Hell, before he got out.

SHRINK. Without cause?

REEVES. Plenty of cause.

SHRINK. What?

REEVES. He *shot* Sgt. Ortiz.

SHRINK. You had no way of knowing —

REEVES. I did.

(Fuck, terrible pain.)

I knew. I knew it would happen. We all knew.

SHRINK. How?

REEVES. He never looked out for himself. It was just a question of time. We should of been looking out for him. *We knew.*

SHRINK. So you should have shot anybody who got out of a car? You think Sgt. Ortiz would have approved of that?

REEVES. He would have been mad, but after he found the gun? He would've thanked me. Put his hand out. Smiled. He'd know I was watching out for him.

SHRINK. You see this in your head a lot.

REEVES. Like that movie you were talking about? Yes, ma'am. It's a good movie. A feel-good movie. You ought to catch it some time.

(Silence. Then —)
SHRINK. You want to kill everybody.
REEVES. *(Amazed!)*
Oh, you figured that out, huh? God, you're smart. That's how you got to be a shrink in the army, right? Because you're so *smart* and can figure things like that out. I want to kill everybody — everybody but you — and what I *do* want to do to you — well, I suspect that falls into the normal category too.
(Then —)
SHRINK. OK, we're done here.
REEVES. *(Leaving.)*
Yes, we are.
(He moves. Stops.)
SHRINK. We're done.
(Then —)
REEVES. This is confidential, right?
SHRINK. No, not right. I told you what I could hear and what I couldn't.
(Silence. Then —)
REEVES. If I had a bullet in my head and I were lying here, you'd feel bad for me?
SHRINK. I would.
REEVES. Do I have to have a bullet in my head to qualify?
(Silence.)
If I were laying here on your floor bleeding from the head, *how long* would you feel bad for me?
(No response.)
Because — out there — they put a bullet in me — they'd celebrate for a month. A year. Fuck. Forever. They kill me, they get to go to God, directly to God, do not stop at any checkpoints. When those construction workers got killed — they hung their body parts from the bridge and they danced their asses off for days. Now you want to talk about sympathy — I've got all kinds of sympathy for that because that is *exactly* how I feel about them. We want each other dead. Now you — you've got all the sympathy in the world for a dying sergeant — fuck — ANYBODY CAN FEEL SYMPATHY FOR THE GOOD GUY. He doesn't *need* your sympathy. He's got a wife and a kid for that. But that guy who shot him — I want to fucking kill him over and over. That's what goes on in my head and you've got no sympathy for that. "Don't tell me that. You're on your

59

own with that" and you know what that means? You've got no sympathy for the one thing that *needs* it here and I don't want to make him an excuse. I think I've *always* wanted to kill everybody. Him dying just makes me think I'm finally going to do it.

(Brief, brief moment. Then, pissed —)

SHRINK. You're a killer.

REEVES. Yes, ma'am. I have killed.

SHRINK. *(Escalating.)*

And it didn't bother you?

REEVES. No, ma'am it did not. That's who I am.

SHRINK. A killer?

REEVES. Yes, ma'am.

SHRINK. Well, killer, did it bother you that you drooled on the sergeant?

REEVES. *(Stung.)*

I wiped it off.

SHRINK. *(Escalating.)*

Why? It didn't bother him.

REEVES. I *wiped* it *off.*

SHRINK. *(Escalating.)*

Why? Did it *bother* you?

REEVES. *You gonna make fun of me for that?*

SHRINK. *Are you going to attack me for trying to help you?*

REEVES. *No, ma'am. Help me.*

SHRINK. *Help me and I will.*

REEVES. *(Exploding.)*

SHIT!

(Reeves weeps. Weeps till he drools. Weeps more. Shrink watches. Then —)

SHRINK. How old are you, soldier?

REEVES. I'm a fucking baby.

(Silence. Then — with compassion —)

SHRINK. Do you think. Do you think the sergeant might have been thinking of his daughter as he was dying?

REEVES. He thought about her all the time. He had her name tattooed on his arm.

SHRINK. So — maybe the drool made sense to him.

REEVES. Ma'am?

SHRINK. I mean, she's a kid, right. Kids drool on their fathers. Maybe it made sense to him. Maybe he thought it was her.

(Reeves takes that in.)
REEVES. I wish it was.
(Then.)
Till he turned into a sack of shit and blood.
(Then.)
Then it was good it was me there and not her.
(Silence. Then —)
SHRINK. I think that's what I was trying to say before.
(Then.)
Sorry.
REEVES. I get it.
(Then.)
It's hard sometimes to —
SHRINK. I get it.
REEVES. I —
(They both get it. Then —)
SHRINK. When was the last time you felt that?
REEVES. What?
SHRINK. That it was good that you were there.
(No response.)
You felt like you were part of his family.
(Silence.)
REEVES. No.
SHRINK. No?
(No.)
REEVES. I felt I was part of him.
(And this is painful, glorious and shameful. Silence. Then —)
SHRINK. When was the last time you felt that?
REEVES. Like I said — when he died.
SHRINK. *(No.)*
Before that?
(Silence.)
You can look at me.
(Nothing.)
Solider.
(Nothing.)
Eyes.
(He looks at her.)
Have you felt that way before?
(Silence. She holds his glance throughout.)

You never— You've never felt that way before.
(Silence.)
You always felt alone?
REEVES. I always figured I felt pretty much the way everybody feels.
(Then.)
That's not right. Is it?
(Then.)
What I felt on the Hummer hood — that's normal. Right?
(No response.)
I'm one of those morons you were talking about.
SHRINK. Morons?
REEVES. Things that are the opposite of themselves.
(Silence. Then —)
SHRINK. Soldier.
REEVES. Ma'am.
SHRINK. I think you've been in Iraq too long.
REEVES. Ma'am, do NOT — do not send me home.
(Then.)
I am begging you. Let me stay.
SHRINK. Why? So you can kill everybody?
(No.)
SHRINK. Why then?
(Truth.)
REEVES. Ma'am, I think being here is my one shot at normal.
(Then.)
What happened? I want that to happen again.
(Then.)
I'd like to feel that a —
(Then, deeply embarrassed.)
Look, let's just forget I ever came in here. Nobody knows but us.
OK? Please. Let's just forget it.
SHRINK. You want to forget this conversation?
REEVES. No, ma'am.
(Then.)
At least not all of it. That thing you said about the. The drool? That
was a nice thing to say. Even if it wasn't true. I'll think about that later.
(She needs a commitment from him. Laying it out —)
SHRINK. Kids drool on their dads. They cry on them too. Kids
cry a lot. Cry till somebody comes to pick them up. Some kids
don't get picked up. Crying doesn't do them much good — so they

stop. Some start again. Some don't. Doesn't matter much one way or the other.
(Then.)
They can't stop crying — we send them home.
(Then.)
They can stop — that's good for me — because I get to recycle them. Either way's OK, but I got to know which way is the soldier's way so they don't end up fucking everybody up.
(Then.)
Are you going to fuck everybody up?
REEVES. *(Honest/amused.)*
Well — I always have.
(Wrong answer. She goes to write him out of the army.)
Can I try that again, ma'am?
SHRINK. Are you going to —
REEVES. No, ma'am.
(Then.)
How about this? I don't want to kill everybody. Just the bad people. Is that normal enough?
(She nods. Enter the Lawyer from the fifth circle.)
LAWYER. Did you ever go back?
REEVES. Told you. I never saw anybody twice till you.
(Then, to the shrink.)
I picked a bad time to go normal, didn't I?
SHRINK. Here. This might help.
(She picks pill bottle up from the stage. Offers them to him.)
REEVES. What are these?
SHRINK. Seroquel. Something to take the edge off.
REEVES. Ma'am, the last thing I want is for the edge to be taken off.
(He takes the pills from her anyway.)
LAWYER. What happened then?
REEVES. She told me to get a good night of sleep.
SHRINK. Try to get a good night of sleep.
LAWYER. When did you see the shrink again?
REEVES. Different shrink. After the dog. See —
(To audience.)
It was the dog that got them upset.

CIRCLE 7: THE TRIAL

REEVES.   CIRCLE SEVEN.   THE TRIAL OF DANIEL EDWARD REEVES.
(Re: the man —)
Lawyer for the Defense.
(The Lawyer from Circle Five defends Daniel who is sitting center. Listening. Weighing. The key element of this scene will appear later — word vs. flesh. We begin with word.)
DEFENSE.   The crime we are discussing only *ended* in Iraq. It began in a recruiting office in Texas.
(Then.)
There — a recruiting officer met a deeply troubled nineteen-year-old with convictions for alcohol, drug abuse, violence. He had a personality disorder and everybody in town knew it. To make his quota, this recruiting office obtained a morals waivers for him, and this disturbed young man was soon strapped up with world-class weaponry to fight in a war so lacking in popular support that an army could not be assembled to fight it — without candidates like this young man.
REEVES.   *(Re: the woman —)*
Lawyer for the Prosecution.
(The woman enters — professionally dressed.)
PROSECUTION.   I'm all for sympathy for the soldier, but mustn't someone speak for the girl.
(Then.)
A cotton dress. I want to speak to you about a cotton dress.
(Then.)
Young girls need protection. The girl we are concerned with — living in a war zone — needed more than most. She had a cotton dress.
(Then.)
She *had* had another defense — her family. But a soldier deprived her of the protection of her family when he herded her father, her mother, and four-year-old sister into the family bedroom and murdered them in cold blood.
(Then.)
This soldier then proceeded from the bedroom to the living room where two of his fellow soldiers were holding the girl on the floor

and — against them — against him — the protection of a cotton dress was not sufficient. This is the crime we are investigating.

DEFENSE.   OK. Let's investigate the crime. Starting with the murder.

(Then.)

Let's look at the weapon.

(He looks around. Finds none.)

We cannot.

(Then.)

Let us investigate the rape. Let's examine the DNA evidence.

(He looks around/nothing.)

None … OK, then. Let's — Let's take a look at that cotton dress.

(Then.)

No dress?

(To the Prosecution.)

Do we ever know if the dress was cotton?

PROSECUTION.   There are photographs.

DEFENSE.   Without a single bit of evidence to back them up — for all we know they could have been taken on a studio backlot.

(Then.)

Strange trial in which there is absolutely no evidence.

PROSECUTION.   There is testimony.

DEFENSE.   There is a flood of testimony.

(To the audience.)

Every bit of it coming from men and women who outrank my client placing every bit of the blame on him — the lowest ranking man involved in this incident.

(Then.)

A ritual was invented in the ancient Near East — not far from where the events we are discussing took place. For terrible crimes, all blame was placed on an animal and the animal was driven into the wilderness to die.

(Then.)

We are more enlightened now. We would never allow an animal's life to be sacrificed. And yet. Our government — from the president on down — is calling for the scapegoating of a young man — the lowest ranking man involved in this admittedly horrifying event.

PROSECUTION.   What we are discussing did not take place in the mythic past, but in the nearly immediate present. It was not a symbolic action. It was not an "event" or an "incident." It was a crime. Very real. Very brutal. And, in it, rank is absolutely immaterial. Nuremberg made that quite clear. A solider of any rank is responsible for his moral choices.

(A moment. Then —)

REEVES. He's my lawyer, but I like her.

(Reeves rises.)

This isn't about me. Go on.

(He changes out of his prison jumpsuit. While the attorneys continue their impassioned words, Reeves strips naked, washes himself and dresses in a clean white T-shirt, distinctive underpants — diaper actually — and new institutional white pants. The trial continues over the physical, ritual transformation of Reeves.)

PROSECUTION. The testimony. Though much of the testimony in this case is compromised, there is one unimpeachable witness — the accused himself. He *told* people he was out to kill.

DEFENSE. No dispute there.

(With some enthusiasm.)

Daniel Reeves told anyone who would listen he intended to kill. He wanted to kill everybody. More specifically, all Iraqis.

(Then.)

To his everlasting credit, he sought help. He went to an army psychiatrist, asked for help, was given unrecorded medication, told to get a good night's sleep and was recycled the next day to patrol the area known as The Triangle of Death. With disastrous consequences. What were his superiors expecting?

PROSECUTION. I want to be careful here.

(Then.)

I too think it is admirable that a troubled soldier sought help. And the army was remiss in not providing more help than it did. No question. However. There is a conclusion to this seeking for help that the Defense does not draw.

(Then.)

The Defense has — condescendingly — portrayed Mr. Reeves as an animal. A goat and that is not fair. Mr. Reeves is a man, a smart young man. He may have been undereducated when he was inducted into the army, but he educated himself along the way. He learned.

(Then.)

He learned some Arabic. Leadership skills. Even moral virtue — loyalty — brotherhood — self-sacrifice. He availed himself of his opportunities and, troubled by his desire to kill, he — sought —

66

help. And the logical conclusion of this is — unfortunately —
(Then.)
He knew what he was planning on doing — was *wrong.*
(Then.)
He *knew* it was wrong.
(Then.)
And he did it *anyway.* This crime deserves — it demands judgment.
DEFENSE. Let's say it does. Who then can judge this man?
(Then.)
And it is at *this* point that Nuremberg becomes instructive. Who
were the judges then? Who was the jury?
(Then.)
They were the ones who said "no." Not in casual conversation, but
with the commitment of their lives. Not the ones who financed the
war with their obedient taxes. Not the ones who have not said no to
this insane useless violence. Who has the right to judge this man?
(Then.)
Anybody who stood in front of a recruiting center and said, "No."
"You can't have them." "Not if this is what you are going to do with
them." "This is not what we do with our young."
(Then.)
If that's who you are — judge. If not — don't. Not even in the
secrecy of your thoughts. You — no — We — We haven't the right.
How could we? We hired him. We paid his salary. We were his
employers.
(As he completes his case, Prosecution takes stage.)
PROSECUTION. This is not — not — about the war. This is
about a young girl.
(Then.)
The Defense wants to tell you who you are in this case, but you already
know. You are the rule of law. You are a young girl's last line of protec-
tion. What her family could not do — what a dress could not do —
you can. The law is in your hands. Her final fate — is in your hands.
(Then.)
The choice is yours. Guilty. Or not? Consider your decision.
*(Reeves stands for a long moment. Long enough for the audience to
make a decision.)*
MAN. CIRCLE EIGHT. THE LAST WORDS OF DANIEL
EDWARD REEVES.

CIRCLE 8: LAST WORDS

Reeves — terrified — attempting to appear confident — stands before the audience at his execution.

REEVES. I've had a good life. Can't complain. I had my war. It was a learning experience. For example —

The Battle of Lepanto was fought in 1571. I have learned that.

Shrinks fuck up your head; lawyers talk; soldiers — they can't keep a secret.

Even if you've got nothing, people still try to take things from you.

I've met a couple of good people, but I don't know how they do it.

In the story about Jesus and the woman? I wonder. I wonder where that demon went when he got driven out. I suspect I'm about to find out. If I wake up and there's sand, I'll know I'm in hell.

Nobody can tell my story because nobody knows it.

How can they?

Nobody ever asks the right questions.

They asked me what I wanted for my last meal. Like I'm thinking about food.

They should have asked me what I wanted to wear.

I did not want to die in a diaper.

This is my story. I did it. I raped her and I killed her family. I wish I didn't but I thought about it and I honestly don't see how anything could have been different.

I don't have a daughter.

I regret that.

I think I could have given better than I got, but I learned how a little late.

That also seems to be the story of my life.

The Battle of Lepanto took place in 1571 but somehow I fought in it.

Seems to me that people do not learn a lot.

Seems to me that I have learned more than most.
(After some thought.)
That's about it.
(Silence.)
WOMAN. CIRCLE NINE. INFERNO.
(All other cast leave.)
(Reeves — for the first time — is alone.)

CIRCLE 9: INFERNO

Quietly.

Body — perfectly still.

Heart and mind electrically, passionately alive within the physical stillness.

REEVES. Where am I?

I hate waking up not knowing where I.

No sand.

Well.

That's good.

(Noticing.)
People. Looking at me.

Where am?

On a couch. Can't move. Strapped down. Am I in a hospital? Did
I. Did I wreck the car?

I need the car.

Mr. Reeves, in all probability you will never.
(Remembering where he is.)
Oh.

So that's.

They didn't find the vein. Stuck me five times and they still couldn't
find the vein. What was it? Potassium chloride right into the muscle. *Fucking amateurs. I knew this would happen. I fucking knew.
Fucking knew I'd wake up. I.*

No. No act. Go like him. Quiet.
(Silence.)
Anybody asks does it hurt?
(Silence. Then, in terrible pain —)
Hurts.

Sharks.

Coyotes.

Don't cry.
Pointless.
(Perfect clarity and tears.)

Nobody's coming.

If my head was cut off, they'd come. Go ahead. Do it. *Hell, bury me up to my neck in sand and stone me too.* No. No act. He was right. No act. Go like him.

He looked at me. Saw something. Something good.

That was my life. Not twenty years. Not ten months. Five minutes on a hummer hood. That was enough. Go like him. No words at all. *(Silence. Then — terrible pain —)*
Muscles inside out.

Don't fight it. Give in to it. People are supposed to die. Die. *(Silence.)*
Can't.

One more thing I can't. *(To audience —)*
Help me. *(No one moves.)*
Don't cry. She cried. Don't go like her screaming and crying. Eyes, soldier. He saw. In me. Something.

She saw. Lifted her head and saw. Saw me come in. Last person in the world.

Sa'idny. She said Sa'idny.
How am I supposed to know what that meant. *(His own pain.)*
Christ help me. Help. Me. *(Silence.)*
Cavalry isn't coming.

The cavalry isn't coming, darling. You know what I came to.

Sa'idny. Sa'idny. What did I feel? Not much. Very little. She felt — very little. Very. Soft. Felt her. No munitions strapped on.

Got to do it. What I came to do. I got people looking at me. Got

to get it done. Help me, darling.
(His pain.)
Don't fight. Oh, Christ. Don't fight. She fought. Fought them. Fought me.

Looked in her eyes.

That was my mistake. Wasn't it.

Her eyes.

Saw.

I knew.

Right away.

Wrong place.

Should've left.

Couldn't.

Can't now.

People watching.

Got to do it. Put your head down and do.

Head down.

Eyes closed.

But I knew. Knew then. Right away.

No.

No Hummer hood for me.

Army of one.

Forever.

What would he say if.

Felt tears.

On my face.

Not crying but.

Tears.

In my eyes.

Her tears.

In my eyes.

Pain of the.
(Unendurable.)
War over.
(A moment.)
Dishonorable discharge.
(A moment.)
She saw.

Me.

Last one in the world.

Who could. Help.

Sa'idny.

No act. I knew. I knew what she said. I'm smart. Sa'idny. I knew
what she said. Help me. Help me. She said — Help. Me.
(To her —)
Show me. Show me how.
(She speaks.)
"Halini A'ish."

What?

"Halini A'ish."

And I thought no. You don't want that. That's not what you want.

Your family is gone.

Halini A'ishhhhhhh. Let me live.

You've been with me. No one will touch you.

Halini A'isssssssh. Let me live.

Even if they don't stone you, you'd always be alone. You don't know what that's like. You don't want that. You've never been. No, it's better this way.

Halini A —

Bang.

I ended it.

Sympathetic reaction.
(Then — terrible pain.)
This is it. This is death. Has to be. Can't get worse.
(Silence. Then —)
Worse.
(Then —)
Won't shout.
Feel it. Feel what she.
(Silence.)
Don't shout.

Be him.

For once.

At the end.

No more words.

Won't speak again.

Silence.
(Against his will — her voice —)
Halini A'ish.

Oh, God.

Let.

Me.

(Blackout. A breathing out of a spirit into the darkness.)

End of Play

PRODUCTION NOTES

Doubling — The play is written for doubling. This isn't an attempt to save money by cutting cast size. I almost always use doubling. One of the things that makes theater work, in my opinion, is seeing the infinite possibilities of our lives in the persons of actors. Doubling makes us feel that what Shakespeare says is true — that one man or woman in his or her time can be many things. We always need to be reminded of that.

Beyond that, in *9 Circles*, I believe that the theatricality of doubling Reeves' visitors reinforces the singularity of Reeves.

I have no preference for how the doubling works, but some thought should be given to costume changes. You don't want to sit too long in transitions while an actor is switching from character to character.

Circle 1 — A thought about the couch speech and Reeves. It's not meant to be poetic. While researching the first circle I came across an article in a medical journal about the nature of wounds in the Iraq war. I found myself looking at the pictures without understanding what I was seeing. It took me a while to realize that the doctors were actually holding the limbs of a living soldier. The skin, bone and muscle were so shredded that initially I saw what Reeves describes. In other pictures, limbs were torn in ways that looked like shark bites. In this scene, I wasn't trying to write poetry for Reeves. I was just trying to describe what I saw.

Circle 2 — There are two instances of nudity in the show. This is the first. If you can do the nudity, I request that you do. In this instance, everything is taken from him and, to feel that, it helps if we see that.

I want to thank Jim Carpenter from the Marin Theater Company production for adlibbing the line, "Son, you can keep anything that isn't stamped PROPERTY OF THE UNITED STATES ARMY." We were trying to come up with the exact right line to cue the change and Jim came through with it.

Circle 3 — "It doesn't make any sense." Jim Carpenter again. Jim found an interesting moment in this scene that is worth mentioning. His military lawyer was very precise, very restrained, but he built to an unexpectedly emotional moment on the line, "It doesn't make any sense." At that moment, the lawyer's very great love of the military crashed up against reality and gave the scene unexpected heart.

Circle 4 — The gospel passages are Mark 7:25 and Matthew 15:21. People initially don't believe me when I tell them the story, but it's there — and it's a shock that it is.

The gospel story is repeated several times by Reeves at the end of the scene. Use as much of this text as is needed to complete putting Reeves in restraints and no more. The goal of this material is to give Reeves actable material to reach the emotional state he needs to be in to start Circle 5.

Circle 5 — As the **civilian lawyer** thinks trials are wonderful, I think the civilian lawyer is wonderful. He does, however, have a great deal to say and can wear out his welcome if he breaks the scene into too many small units. He thinks in long, argumentative sequences. In general, the longer he can sustain a growing line of thought, the better. He then explodes through the thought into moments of earned silence — as, for example, the silence that follows the finger on Reeves' forehead and the repeated moments after the "prove it's."

Circle 6 — Purgatorio — Canto XXVII.

Circle 7 — The trial. It's worth noting that these speeches are summations at the end of a trial — not opening statements. They are the final chances these lawyers have to make their points. Though they are laying out their cases in a reasoned way, this should not get in the way of their passion for their causes. There is a drive to their words.

The second instance of nudity is the opposite of the first. Reeves is not forced into this moment. He is consciously preparing himself for what is to come. This preparation gives a sense of the young man's youth and utter vulnerability. And, in contrast to all the words words words of the lawyers, it gives us a strong sense that the action that we are approaching is finally a physical one — as the inciting action of the play was. It also invites us into a private world — where we will stay for the rest of the play.

Circle 8 — Summing up a life. In the Marin production, Craig Marker — who played Reeves — did an extraordinary thing in a rehearsal run-through of this scene. Kent Nicholson, the director, and I had known from the start that we wanted to do something interesting with all of the emblems that the various characters had left behind in the scenes, but we didn't know exactly what. We had discussed this with the cast, and in a run, without telling us before he did it, Craig slowly gathered all the elements together as he spoke. He put the military boots down center and assembled the other items around the boots to create a soldier's memorial grave. He then took the beer bottle and poured imagined contents over the grave. It was a remarkable rehearsal moment and we kept it in the show.

I thought of adding it to the stage directions, but decided against it because, in other productions, the simplicity of Reeves simply addressing the audience — in its dual role as theater audience and witness to the execution — is equally moving. But it was a great moment and I want to mention it here.

Circle 9 — Patrick Adams — to whom this text is dedicated — was handed the text of Circle 9 shortly before he had to go on stage and do it. He had almost no preparation time before he performed it — breathtakingly — in the first workshop of the play at Ojai Playwrights Conference.

I had submitted a complete script to the Ojai Playwrights Conference of a play called *How to Write a New Book for The Bible* and then, as an afterthought, I sent Robert Egan, the artistic director, the first five circles of *9 Circles* — which was all I had. Bob called me up and said he'd be glad to do either piece but he would prefer *9 Circles* as completing fragmentary text was very much in the spirit of the mission of the Conference. I said, "Fine, as long as we can call the finished piece *5 Circles* if I can't finish it." He said, generously, "Come."

I arrived with seven and a half circles and worked unsuccessfully — between rehearsals of what we had — to finish the piece. The day before we had to present, Hal Brooks, the director, Patrick Adams and Beth Blickers, my agent — sat me down with my piles of notes on 8 and 9 and asked me to tell them what I wanted out of the end of the play. It was a clarifying moment. They listened patiently and, when I finished, they said, "Go home and write it down."

I spent that night writing and rewriting the fragmentary, broken words that make up the 9th circle.

The following morning shortly before we were to present, I handed the text to Patrick and said, "Cross out anything you don't think you need."

Hal and Patrick went through it briefly and then we presented.

The reading of the first eight circles had been electrifying. Then — as the other cast members exited — Patrick was left on stage — perfectly still — a blinding white light carving out a space in the darkness for him.

Patrick brought an absolute concentration to each moment that made any movement superfluous. He gave an astonishing performance and this remains my preferred version of the scene — standing absolutely still — alive to each moment.

Running time — In my experience, *9 Circles* plays best without intermission and comes in — once the run settles in — between 100 and 105 minutes.

Thank you for reading this play and, if you produce it, profound thanks. *9 Circles* means a lot to me. I am very grateful whenever and wherever it finds its way into the world.

PROPERTY LIST

Army boots
Discharge orders
Pen
Empty beer bottle
List of charges
Military hat
Briefcase
Bible
Notes
Bottle of pills

SOUND EFFECTS

Gavel

NEW PLAYS

★ **MOTHERHOOD OUT LOUD by Leslie Ayvazian, Brooke Berman, David Cale, Jessica Goldberg, Beth Henley, Lameece Issaq, Claire LaZebnik, Lisa Loomer, Michele Lowe, Marco Pennette, Theresa Rebeck, Luanne Rice, Annie Weisman and Cheryl L. West, conceived by Susan R. Rose and Joan Stein.** When entrusting the subject of motherhood to such a dazzling collection of celebrated American writers, what results is a joyous, moving, hilarious, and altogether thrilling theatrical event. "Never fails to strike both the funny bone and the heart." *–BackStage.* "Packed with wisdom, laughter, and plenty of wry surprises." *–TheaterMania.* [1M, 3W] ISBN: 978-0-8222-2589-8

★ **COCK by Mike Bartlett.** When John takes a break from his boyfriend, he accidentally meets the girl of his dreams. Filled with guilt and indecision, he decides there is only one way to straighten this out. "[A] brilliant and blackly hilarious feat of provocation." *–Independent.* "A smart, prickly and rewarding view of sexual and emotional confusion." *–Evening Standard.* [3M, 1W] ISBN: 978-0-8222-2766-3

★ **F. Scott Fitzgerald's THE GREAT GATSBY adapted for the stage by Simon Levy.** Jay Gatsby, a self-made millionaire, passionately pursues the elusive Daisy Buchanan. Nick Carraway, a young newcomer to Long Island, is drawn into their world of obsession, greed and danger. "Levy's combination of narration, dialogue and action delivers most of what is best in the novel." *–Seattle Post-Intelligencer.* "A beautifully crafted interpretation of the 1925 novel which defined the Jazz Age." *–London Free Press.* [5M, 4W] ISBN: 978-0-8222-2727-4

★ **LONELY, I'M NOT by Paul Weitz.** At an age when most people are discovering what they want to do with their lives, Porter has been married and divorced, earned seven figures as a corporate "ninja," and had a nervous breakdown. It's been four years since he's had a job or a date, and he's decided to give life another shot. "Critic's pick!" *–NY Times.* "An enjoyable ride." *–NY Daily News.* [3M, 3W] ISBN: 978-0-8222-2734-2

★ **ASUNCION by Jesse Eisenberg.** Edgar and Vinny are not racist. In fact, Edgar maintains a blog condemning American imperialism, and Vinny is three-quarters into a Ph.D. in Black Studies. When Asuncion becomes their new roommate, the boys have a perfect opportunity to demonstrate how open-minded they truly are. "Mr. Eisenberg writes lively dialogue that strikes plenty of comic sparks." *–NY Times.* "An almost ridiculously enjoyable portrait of slacker trauma among would-be intellectuals." *–Newsday.* [2M, 2W] ISBN: 978-0-8222-2630-7

DRAMATISTS PLAY SERVICE, INC.
440 Park Avenue South, New York, NY 10016 212-683-8960 Fax 212-213-1539
postmaster@dramatists.com www.dramatists.com

NEW PLAYS

★ THE PICTURE OF DORIAN GRAY by Roberto Aguirre-Sacasa, based on the novel by Oscar Wilde. Preternaturally handsome Dorian Gray has his portrait painted by his college classmate Basil Hallwood. When their mutual friend Henry Wotton offers to include it in a show, Dorian makes a fateful wish—that his portrait should grow old instead of him—and strikes an unspeakable bargain with the devil. [5M, 2W] ISBN: 978-0-8222-2590-4

★ THE LYONS by Nicky Silver. As Ben Lyons lies dying, it becomes clear that he and his wife have been at war for many years, and his impending demise has brought no relief. When they're joined by their children all efforts at a sentimental goodbye to the dying patriarch are soon abandoned. "Hilariously frank, clear-sighted, compassionate and forgiving." –NY Times. "Mordant, dark and rich." –Associated Press. [3M, 3W] ISBN: 978-0-8222-2659-8

★ STANDING ON CEREMONY by Mo Gaffney, Jordan Harrison, Moisés Kaufman, Neil LaBute, Wendy MacLeod, José Rivera, Paul Rudnick, and Doug Wright, conceived by Brian Shnipper. Witty, warm and occasionally wacky, these plays are vows to the blessings of equality, the universal challenges of relationships and the often hilarious power of love. "CEREMONY puts a human face on a hot-button issue and delivers laughter and tears rather than propaganda." –BackStage. [3M, 3W] ISBN: 978-0-8222-2654-3

★ ONE ARM by Moisés Kaufman, based on the short story and screenplay by Tennessee Williams. Ollie joins the Navy and becomes the lightweight boxing champion of the Pacific Fleet. Soon after, he loses his arm in a car accident, and he turns to hustling to survive. "[A] fast, fierce, brutally beautiful stage adaptation." –NY Magazine. "A fascinatingly lurid, provocative and fatalistic piece of theater." –Variety. [7M, 1W] ISBN: 978-0-8222-2564-5

★ AN ILIAD by Lisa Peterson and Denis O'Hare. A modern-day retelling of Homer's classic. Poetry and humor, the ancient tale of the Trojan War and the modern world collide in this captivating theatrical experience. "Shocking, glorious, primal and deeply satisfying." –Time Out NY. "Explosive, altogether breathtaking." –Chicago Sun-Times. [1M] ISBN: 978-0-8222-2687-1

★ THE COLUMNIST by David Auburn. At the height of the Cold War, Joe Alsop is the nation's most influential journalist, beloved, feared and courted by the Washington world. But as the '60s dawn and America undergoes dizzying change, the intense political dramas Joe is embroiled in become deeply personal as well. "Intensely satisfying." –Bloomberg News. [5M, 2W] ISBN: 978-0-8222-2699-4

DRAMATISTS PLAY SERVICE, INC.
440 Park Avenue South, New York, NY 10016 212-683-8960 Fax 212-213-1539
postmaster@dramatists.com www.dramatists.com

NEW PLAYS

★ **BENGAL TIGER AT THE BAGHDAD ZOO by Rajiv Joseph.** The lives of two American Marines and an Iraqi translator are forever changed by an encounter with a quick-witted tiger who haunts the streets of war-torn Baghdad. "[A] boldly imagined, harrowing and surprisingly funny drama." *–NY Times.* "Tragic yet darkly comic and highly imaginative." *–CurtainUp.* [5M, 2W] ISBN: 978-0-8222-2565-2

★ **THE PITMEN PAINTERS by Lee Hall, inspired by a book by William Feaver.** Based on the triumphant true story, a group of British miners discover a new way to express themselves and unexpectedly become art-world sensations. "Excitingly ambiguous, in-the-moment theater." *–NY Times.* "Heartfelt, moving and deeply politicized." *–Chicago Tribune.* [5M, 2W] ISBN: 978-0-8222-2507-2

★ **RELATIVELY SPEAKING by Ethan Coen, Elaine May and Woody Allen.** In TALKING CURE, Ethan Coen uncovers the sort of insanity that can only come from family. Elaine May explores the hilarity of passing in GEORGE IS DEAD. In HONEYMOON MOTEL, Woody Allen invites you to the sort of wedding day you won't forget. "Firecracker funny." *–NY Times.* "A rollicking good time." *–New Yorker.* [8M, 7W] ISBN: 978-0-8222-2394-8

★ **SONS OF THE PROPHET by Stephen Karam.** If to live is to suffer, then Joseph Douaihy is more alive than most. With unexplained chronic pain and the fate of his reeling family on his shoulders, Joseph's health, sanity, and insurance premium are on the line. "Explosively funny." *–NY Times.* "At once deep, deft and beautifully made." *–New Yorker.* [5M, 3W] ISBN: 978-0-8222-2597-3

★ **THE MOUNTAINTOP by Katori Hall.** A gripping reimagination of events the night before the assassination of the civil rights leader Dr. Martin Luther King, Jr. "An ominous electricity crackles through the opening moments." *–NY Times.* "[A] thrilling, wild, provocative flight of magical realism." *–Associated Press.* "Crackles with theatricality and a humanity more moving than sainthood." *–NY Newsday.* [1M, 1W] ISBN: 978-0-8222-2603-1

★ **ALL NEW PEOPLE by Zach Braff.** Charlie is 35, heartbroken, and just wants some time away from the rest of the world. Long Beach Island seems to be the perfect escape until his solitude is interrupted by a motley parade of misfits who show up and change his plans. "Consistently and sometimes sensationally funny." *–NY Times.* "A morbidly funny play about the trendy new existential condition of being young, adorable, and miserable." *–Variety.* [2M, 2W] ISBN: 978-0-8222-2562-1

DRAMATISTS PLAY SERVICE, INC.
440 Park Avenue South, New York, NY 10016 212-683-8960 Fax 212-213-1539
postmaster@dramatists.com www.dramatists.com

NEW PLAYS

★ **CLYBOURNE PARK by Bruce Norris.** WINNER OF THE 2011 PULITZER PRIZE AND 2012 TONY AWARD. Act One takes place in 1959 as community leaders try to stop the sale of a home to a black family. Act Two is set in the same house in the present day as the now predominantly African-American neighborhood battles to hold its ground. "Vital, sharp-witted and ferociously smart." –*NY Times.* "A theatrical treasure…Indisputably, uproariously funny." –*Entertainment Weekly.* [4M, 3W] ISBN: 978-0-8222-2697-0

★ **WATER BY THE SPOONFUL by Quiara Alegría Hudes.** WINNER OF THE 2012 PULITZER PRIZE. A Puerto Rican veteran is surrounded by the North Philadelphia demons he tried to escape in the service. "This is a very funny, warm, and yes uplifting play." –*Hartford Courant.* "The play is a combination poem, prayer and app on how to cope in an age of uncertainty, speed and chaos." –*Variety.* [4M, 3W] ISBN: 978-0-8222-2716-8

★ **RED by John Logan.** WINNER OF THE 2010 TONY AWARD. Mark Rothko has just landed the biggest commission in the history of modern art. But when his young assistant, Ken, gains the confidence to challenge him, Rothko faces the agonizing possibility that his crowning achievement could also become his undoing. "Intense and exciting." –*NY Times.* "Smart, eloquent entertainment." –*New Yorker.* [2M] ISBN: 978-0-8222-2483-9

★ **VENUS IN FUR by David Ives.** Thomas, a beleaguered playwright/director, is desperate to find an actress to play Vanda, the female lead in his adaptation of the classic sadomasochistic tale *Venus in Fur.* "Ninety minutes of good, kinky fun." –*NY Times.* "A fast-paced journey into one man's entrapment by a clever, vengeful female." –*Associated Press.* [1M, 1W] ISBN: 978-0-8222-2603-1

★ **OTHER DESERT CITIES by Jon Robin Baitz.** Brooke returns home to Palm Springs after a six-year absence and announces that she is about to publish a memoir dredging up a pivotal and tragic event in the family's history—a wound they don't want reopened. "Leaves you feeling both moved and gratifyingly sated." –*NY Times.* "A genuine pleasure." –*NY Post.* [2M, 3W] ISBN: 978-0-8222-2605-5

★ **TRIBES by Nina Raine.** Billy was born deaf into a hearing family and adapts brilliantly to his family's unconventional ways, but it's not until he meets Sylvia, a young woman on the brink of deafness, that he finally understands what it means to be understood. "A smart, lively play." –*NY Times.* "[A] bright and boldly provocative drama." –*Associated Press.* [3M, 2W] ISBN: 978-0-8222-2751-9

DRAMATISTS PLAY SERVICE, INC.
440 Park Avenue South, New York, NY 10016 212-683-8960 Fax 212-213-1539
postmaster@dramatists.com www.dramatists.com